From Trisha to Nirvaan

A Journey from Desire to Liberation

Mukundan

Published by **Shambhabi - The Third Eye Imprint,**
A 10/ 1, Amarabati,
Sodepur, Kolkata – 700110
India

Price: Rs. One hundred and eighty only. (Rs.180/-)

"What lies behind us and what lies before us are tiny matters compared to what lies within us..."[3]

~ Oliver Wendell Holmes

Acknowledgements

I thank Sri.Chettur Radhakrishnan for the exemplary foreword he has written for this book. He has left no stones unturned in bringing out the essence of the book in a very apt way. My salutations to him.

This book would not have been published but for the kind and generous heart of Dr. Kiriti Sengupta of Shambabi — The Third Eye Imprint. I am beholden to him and Shambabi Publications for bringing out the publication in an excellent manner.

Last but not the least my infinite thanks to God Almighty for showering the light for the success of this book by making me an instrument of His will.

Foreword

"Conquer the world with your spirituality" was the clarion call echoing for decades across the continents ever since the dawn of 20th century, uttered then by the greatest intellect of our motherland after Gouthama Buddha, Swami Vivekananda who was also the principle disciple of Sri Ramakrishna Paramahamsa. Despite this, our world had to witness the disastrous effects of two global wars, which have almost shattered the "holy" concept of "world peace." In our country, the cradle of "Shanthi mantratraya" defined as "peace which passeth understanding" by T.S.Eliot, in his "Waste Land", the scene now that presents itself before any impartial observer is a welter of conflicting ideologies amidst drift and restlessness. Now, evidently, quests have evolved for well defined values satisfying the aspirations of all. Our youth have gone restive.

At this juncture, Mr.Mukundan has emerged with a quiet resolve to retrieve the lost equilibrium of morals, through his book "From Trtisha to Nirvaan", which appears as a rain cloud during "Agninakshatra" in peak dry summer. I feel his effort is a spontaneous outburst of deep commitment to the society, especially to the youth folk, now lying dormant in the innermost recesses of his heart. The work distinctly reflects the suppressed grief and discontentment in his mind.

The book is a compilation of some essays with high philosophical content. Spread on the essay portions, we come across a wide variety of short stories and events well supporting the doctrines and ample anecdotes from even Christian and Buddhist literatures. By seeing the profuse inclusion of short stories, to be frank, my assessment goes to the extent of saying that Mr. Mukundan is addicted to story-telling. He has no intention other than elucidating each and every mythological concept with an absolute confidence in inculcating the virtues of truth, purity and unselfishness and thus equips the new generation to confront the whole universe. Mr. Mukundan has an appeal to the posterity, to partake in the process of nation building. At this context, it seems apt to recall the saying of Jawaharlal Nehru: "We look forward to new ideas, processes, and experiences as we have to build a noble mansion of India, where our children may dwell."

The concept of Yagna is narrated beautifully in Chapter 1, with a relevant quote from Gita (3: 15). It is rather a sequential depiction of evolution thus: Parabrahma (Akasha)—Veda—Karma—Yagna—Rain—Anna—living beings. We can see an almost similar reference in the sloka:

Agnow prastha hoothi
samyagadithyamupathishtathe Adityajjayathe
Vrishti...

(An oblation duly thrown into fire, reaches the sun, from the sun comes the rain, from the rain food, therefrom the living beings (derive their sustenance)") Manu III-76.

Yagna is nothing but expression of gratitude for help received, which is a cardinal virtue. We will be guilty of gross ingratitude if we do not offer first to God, what we eat or wear. The mongoose story from *The Mahabharatha* was told by Vivekananda in his Chicago speeches.

While endorsing the author's view on "Dharmartha kama moksha," I infer as Kama for "Dharmartha" (wealth i.e. Dharma) will finally lead us to salvation (Moksha). Late Paramacharya of Kanchi Peethom explained once, how the prefix 'Kamakoti' is derived from the above dictum.

The author tells the story of "Gajendramoksha", to warn those who are overconfident of their own strength. The elephant thus stands a clear symbol of egotism. Thus man (Gajendra) plays the game of life with family and friends in this world (lake), where he is confronted by death and other miseries. (Crocodile)

The Hindu firmly believes in rebirths based on individual soul's conduct during his sojourn in this world. His existence here is compared to the lives of fauna in the ocean. The author illustrates this theme through a story in Chapter 2.

The author talks about "Thoughtrons" with a peep into the field of science, drawing our attention further to the experiments of Dr.Sreenivasan (Associate Professor of Physics, B A R C) with his Random Event Generator (REG) equipment and closely similar observations in the same field by Roger Penrose.

A virtuous life prepares the mind as a fit instrument of concentration and meditation. One cannot liberate oneself from the trammels of mind and attain immortality.

The author throws light on the manifold virtues of meditation with his profound experience in the field. Nowadays even top executives of "MNC"s are asked to go for compulsory meditation to mitigate stress and strain on occupational hazards.

Mr. Mukundan has made a fair research, of course, for a catchy caption for his new venture *From Trisha to Nirvaan*, an assortment of carefully selected words. There is no greater Guru than your mind. When mind has been purified by prayers and contemplation, it will direct you from within. Earnestness is the best path to nirvana i.e. Immortality. "Let the inner light of lights, my mind, which travels far whether awake or asleep, be full of divine impulse." (Sukla yajurveda xxxiv: 1)

Apart from the framework of his book, when Mr. Mukundan explained to me his strange experience of seeing God, I felt that he had succeeded in ascending the footstool of God, which in other way means the descent of God into his Soul. We all know great men like Gandhiji, Chembai, Vivekananda and Jayadeva had also similar experiences. Strange and inscrutable are the ways of the Lord and how He comes to life of man. Only men must let God come to their life.

The story telling dates back to five or six centuries B.C., right to the times of epics *The Illiad* and *The Odyssey*. There is a distinct transition from sublimity to simplicity where the genre in it can outwit the intricacies of his essays.

It seems Mr. Mukundan has deliberately kept aloof from commercial gimmicks and the spontaneity is appreciable. - "All world is a stage and all men and women merely players".

Now it is the turn of the readers to ruminate and with the earnest hope that they will vindicate my observations, I humbly bow out.

Chettur Radhakrishnan

Dedication

Vanitha, daughter of a very close friend of mine is a mentally challenged girl but ever loving, jovial and friendly in her own way. She is playful and gregarious. When I am with her I am angry at Almighty God for giving this wonderful being such a handicap. Why at all does God make such discrimination in creating human beings? I feel pained when I think about the thousands of children who are mentally challenged like Vanitha. Her main occupation is copying Ramakatha into her notebooks and she enjoys this pastime. One will be amazed at the number of books she has exhausted copying Rama's and Hanuman's stories.

A Brahmin had accidentally killed his cow. He knew that great sin would befall on him. In order to save himself he decided to go to a great Sage's Ashrama and seek his advice. When he reached the hermitage, the sage had gone to take his bath and his disciple asked him what the matter was. The Brahmin told him the sad story of killing his cow accidentally and asked how to exonerate himself from the sin of committing such a heinous crime.The disciple told him it was very easy. All he had to do was to chant the name of Rama four times. The Brahmin went home pleased.When the sage returned from his bath, the disciple told him about the Brahmin's plight and that he had told him to chant the Rama nama four times to save himself from this sin. The Sage suddenly became very angry and showered his wrath on his disciple cursing him to be born as a Kattala or forest dweller. On asking the cause of his sudden outburst the sage replied, "Why did you ask him to chant the Rama Nama four times? Chanting the name once would have sufficed. You don't believe in the great efficacy of the Rama Nama". The disciple asked for the sage's mercy and the sage blessed him saying he would have occasion to chant the Rama Nama for one thousand years and he would become a great Rishi or sage. This Rishi is the one who later became Valmiki, the author of the famous Ramayana.When one can attain immense merit by chanting the Ramanama just once how much a child like Vanitha would be blessed for copying the Ramakatha into numerous note books!

I dedicate this book to Vanitha and unfortunate children like her. May God be kind to them and I am sure that He would shower His infinite blessings unto them.

Preface

There was a householder who used to chant the Panchakshari mantra "Namah Shivayah" all the time. Although he was a great devotee he was always in poverty and led a very pitiable life. One day Ma Parvathi the consort of Shiva told her husband, "Why don't you give something to this ardent devotee of yours? Don't be so cruel." The Lord replied, "Oh, my beloved! There is no use giving anything to this man. He has no Yoga or fate to enjoy wealth. It would be futile." But Parvathi Devi insisted that he give something. So the Lord made a bag of gold coins and put it on one side of the way where the man was walking and coming. The bag was very attractive and shining. The man as he came the way and was approaching the bag turned his head towards the sky chanting the Lord's name unaware or not noticing the bag of gold coins and walked away, not even casting his eyes on the bag. He was not destined to enjoy the bounty. So the wise man says it should be written on your head while you are born that you are slated to enjoy anything. Only then you can live with it or enjoy it. Even Lord Shiva had to go begging with a bowl in the form of a skull in his hand when his stars were unfavourable. It is said: "What is fated cannot be blotted." But can everybody remain idle thinking that what is fated is to happen and he need not try for anything? The most important thing is to have faith and never to give up trying. We ourselves can change our destiny. It is said in Sanskrit "Utsahinam Purushasimham Upaithi Laksmi" i.e Goddess Lakshmi, the Goddess of wealth, blesses one who is industrious and ever making efforts. This book will introduce you to many new strains of thoughts on the fundamental tenets of many of the Bhagavad Gita slokas. It will also help you to shed off some of the bad habits you have acquired in your life time.I would exhort the reader to have a positive and open mind while going through this book. I have included many stories that are seldom heard and read anywhere. I hope this book will be true to the title of the book *From Trisha to Nirvaan.*

In *The Bible*, Jesus Christ narrates the story of the sower of seeds. When he sowed the seeds some of them fell on the wayside and the birds ate them up. Some of them fell among thorns and could not grow due to the thorns. Some of them fell on plain rock and were destroyed in no time by the scorching heat.Some seeds fell on fertile soil and were nourished by sunshine and water.They grew to blossom and yielded good harvest. While enquiring on the meaning of what he told, Jesus Christ explained that the seeds were God's teachings revealed to humanity in various ways. Some of the teachings were heard by men but they were influenced by the wicked people and perished. The second type of seeds were men who heard the teachings but could not assimilate the true meaning of the teachings and they withered without yielding any result.The third type of seeds were men who could understand and assimilate the true meaning of the teachings and they made good use of it and imbibed the whole teachings to their coming generations and it did plenty of good to the whole world.This was the bountiful harvest. I pray that we all fall into the third category of men and do good things aplenty to the whole world community.

May this book be a source of Bliss to the readers in the same measure as the pleasure, happiness and satisfaction I derived in creating it.

Mukundan

Chapter I

Yagna & Its Benefits

I would like to start this book with this prayer of St: Francis of Assissi.

Lord make me an instrument of your peace
Where there is hatred let me sow love;
Where there is injury, pardon;
Where there is doubt, faith;
Where there is despair, hope;
Where there is darkness, light;
And where there is sadness, joy;

O Divine master, grant that I may not so much seek
To be consoled as to console;
To be understood as to understand;
To be loved, as to love;
For it is in giving that we receive;
It is in pardoning, that we are pardoned
And it is in dying that we are born to eternal light.

The untold sufferings, starvation and health hazards that Swami Vivekananda and his group of sanyasins underwent cannot be described truly by any human words. Their indefatigable efforts were to ease Mother India in the garb of its poor millions from miseries and calamities. The same sincere work is being undertaken by Matha Amritanandamayi Math and The Art of Living Foundation. There are also other innumerable organizations and N.G.O.s undertaking philanthropic causes and you find God's hands extending support and succor to the poor and downtrodden. It is God who prompts us to do something and without His will there is nought.

What can an average Indian do under similar circumstances? We are all endowed with intelligence, education to support it and our day to day needs are met without much pecuniary difficulties. What could be our part in this great task of nation building? Most ordinary people say we do not have any part to play and are not bothered with what happens beyond their human vision or perception. But can we constructively do something for the nation building? First of all what do you mean by Nation Building? Is it constructing huge multiplexes, star hotels, shopping malls in the cities that we call Nation Building? Our strength is in the teaming masses and the masses are in the villages.It is our first and foremost duty to see that every citizen gets his rightful share of at least one square meal a day. The government has the bounden duty to accomplish this task.

We, as the more blessed citizens have the onerous task of assisting in this noble and great endeavour. What can we do sitting in our cosy homes? First of all let us realize the fact that there are millions of people who are less fortunate than us. We can do a small sacrifice for them. We might be indulging in the most luxurious living, consuming unwanted rich food compelling ourselves to devour. When we are concerned for the poor, when we have the feeling that we can also do something for the poor, let us have a frugal meal at least once in a while thinking about their predicament. If you can sacrifice or forgo that much for them it is a great thing and if it is done for the sake of God that sacrifice is a Yagna. Something sacrificed for God's Sake is a Yagna-something you are forsaking for Him. And that Yagna is not something unimportant. Because Bhgawan says in *The Bhagavad Gita* Chapter 3, slokas 14 and 15

Annad Bhavanthi Bhuthani, Parjanyat anna
sambvah
Yagnad bhavathi parjanyo Yagna
karmasamudbhavah

Meaning: from food beings come, from rain is food produced, from Yagna rain proceeds Yagna is born of karma.

Karma brahmodbhavam viddhiBrahmakshara
samudbhavam
Tasmat sarvagatham Brahma Nithyam Yagne
prathishtitham.

Meaning: Know Karma to have risen from *The Vedas* and *Vedas* from the imperishable. The all pervading *Veda* is therefore ever centred in Yagna.

Anything is Yagna. Your chanting the God's name. Your prayer is Yagna. Anything you do religiously, regularly can be considered Yagna if it is done for God's sake. So your having a frugal meal at least once in a while and doing it for the good of the whole world thinking about God becomes a great Yagna. So much good comes out of it. You need not bother whether the other person is doing it. Your individual effort in that line would benefit you knowingly or unknowingly in this birth itself or in the births hereafter.

If a million people are doing such a sacrifice or Yagna see the amount of food and related materials it saves for the world and the pressure on the environment is lessened. It brings more harmony into life, indirectly brings more rains and more hungry stomachs can be filled. Here it is pertinent to quote the lines in Chapter 4, Sloka 31 of *The Bhagavad Gita:*

Nayam lokostayagnasya kuthonya kurusathama

Meaning: This world is not for the person who does not do sacrifice, how then the other the best of Kurus? So it is best for everyone to do some sacrifice or Yagna. *The Bhagavad Gita* Chapter 3 Sloka 13 is very assertive that a man should offer Yagna-a prtion of his food to the deities and then only partake of his food.

Yagnashishtasinah santo Muchyanthe
sarvakilbhishaihi
Bhunjathe the thvagham Papah Ye
pachanthyatmakaranat

Meaning: The good who eat the remains of Yagna are freed from all sins.But the sinful ones who cook food only for themselves, they verily eat sin.

A Deity can also be any fellow being, whom you consider as God. The Indian cultural tradition treats a guest as God. They say, "Athithi Devo Bhava."

A story from *The Mahabharatha* is very relevant here. Yudhishtira performed a great Rajasuya Yagna. All the revered ones hailed it as an unparalleled one. But there came a strange looking mongoose with half of its body in golden colour to the court. He rolled over in the Yagna place and ridiculed all the ones who had extolled the Yagna.On questioning him he narrated a blessed incident. There was a poor pious Brahmin teacher in a nearby village living with his wife, son and daughter-in-law. Once there was acute famine in the village and the family had to go without food for days together.But the Brahmin somehow continued his teaching classes. One day one of his pupils presented him with some flour. The Brahmin thanked God and his wife made four loaves of bread for four of them to eat.As they prayed to God and sat down to eat there was a knock on the door. A strange guest arrived saying he was very hungry and he wanted something to eat. The poor Brahmin was an extremely pious man, so he gave his bread to the guest.After eating the bread the guest's hunger could not be appeased so he asked for more. The dutiful wife of the Brahmin gave her share. Still the stranger looked famished.Although they had not been able to get anything to eat for about a week, the son who understood his father's predicament offered his bread to the stranger. But the stranger would not be contented. He wanted more. The Brahmin who had an ideal daughter-in-law, offered her bread also to the guest. The guest was so pleased with their hospitality and devotion that he revealed his identity.He was none other than Lord Narayana Himself. And at that instant their dilapidated hut turned into a golden house. It was at that time that the mongoose happened to enter the house through a hole. When one half of his body had penetrated the house everything in the house transformed into gold and so half of his body became golden.

The mongoose narrated this story in Yudhishtira's Rajasuya Yagna assembly and told them since then he had been attending all the Yagnas to see whether the other half of his body also would turn into gold.But it never happened there. So before partaking food it is only apt to offer it to somebody, either the Gods or a guest and it becomes a Yagna. A sacrifice done rightly is a Yagna.

Man becomes a true man when he dreams and strives for a higher life. Every living creature is potentially divine. The best way to become a better soul is to do everything for God's sake. Bhagawan has said in *The Bhagavad Gita* Chapter 9, Sloka 27:

*Yad karoshi yadashnasi yajjuhoshi dadasi yat
Yad tapasyasi Kaunteya tad kurushva madarpanam*

Meaning: Whatever you do, whatever you eat, whatever you offer in sacrifice, whatever you gift away, whatever austerity you practice, oh! Kauntheya, do it as an offering to me.

If one is in the habit of smoking or drinking by indulging in a habit excessively, one is injuring the God in one. You are doing untold harm to the God in us. When we become aware that we are injuring ourselves our conscience pricks and we might get a control over the bad habit.

The Bhagavad Gita Chapter 9 slokas 30 and 31 give solace to the sinful one:

*Api ched suduracharo bhajathe mamananyabhak
Sadhurevasa mandhavya samyak vyavasathohi sa*

Meaning: Even if the man of most sinful conduct worships me with undeviated devotion, he must be considered to be righteous because he is rightly resolved.

*Kshipram bhavathi dharmatma shashwachanthim
nigachathi
Kauntheya pratijanihi na Me bhakthaha pranasyathi*

Meaning: Soon does he become a man of righteousness and obtains lasting peace. Know for certain that my devotee never perishes.

Once a very perturbed householder approached Sri Ramakrishna Paramahamsa and told him he was not able to concentrate in his prayers. Bhagawan asked him what was it that caused the hindrance to his prayers. He said he was very much attached to his young goat and every time he tried to concentrate the goat would come in his mind. Sri Ramakrishna told the man to visualize God in his Goat and pray. Soon the man was able to overcome the difficulty because he followed the Saint's advice.

If you are unduly bothered or attached to a thing like smoking or drinking and you find you are not able to progess in your spiritual practices, you deeply concentrate and ponder over the thing. You have an ardent entreatment when you ponder and you will be able to get rid of the fascination. One should not fear to think about anything.It is the fearless who achieve the goal. According to the Hindu Shastra there are four purusharthas. *Dharma*, *Kama*, *Artha* and *Moksha*, which one has to achieve in life.You can indulge in anything, say, *Artha* and *Kama*, but, always have *Dharma* in mind.

Once there was utter chaos in the three worlds. The human beings were accumulating wealth unscrupulously for their own needs. The Danavas (Asura or Demons) were indulging in inhuman atrocities and the Devas were indulging in uncontrolled sense indulgences. So it was all chaos and confusion in the three worlds. All three had a feeling of frustration and had a consultation among them and they decided to approach Prajapathi Brahma for a solution.They found Brahma in meditation and so they sat in front of him and started praying.

Suddenly Brahma awoke from his trance and uttered one sullable "Da" and again went into deep meditation.All three the human beings,the danavas and Devas were pleased because they thought they understood what Brahma wanted to convey.The human beings felt that Brahma by uttering the syllable "Da"had told them to do Dana or charity.So they started giving away all their wealth that they had accumulated.The Danavas thought that by uttering "Da"Brahma had instructed them to show Daya or compassion or practice kindness. So they started to show compassion or kindness to all beings. The Devas construed that by uttering "Da" Brahma told them to practice Dama or restraint. So they started to practice restraint or having control on their sensual indulgences. Soon there was peace in the three worlds.In today's world we have to have all three" Dana, Daya and Dama." Then undoubtedly there will be peace pervading the entire world.

Sri Ramakrishna Paramahamsa often told the story of the servant maid. The maid servant does all the work in her employer's house and looks after his children as if they were her own. But in her heart of hearts she knows she has her own house and her own children elsewhere. Her mind is always on them. We should also live in this world like the maid servant. Always thinking our true world is elsewhere. Nothing ever belongs to us here. We will be asked to quit at any time. This our world is not permanant. And that is the truth. Whatever belongings or treasures we have are His. We are just custodians for a short while. He will take it all at any time. We find that suddenly a poor man becomes rich and starts living in a palatial house with servants and orderlies. At the same time an affluent man staying in the palace finds himself in trouble and very next day he loses everything and sometimes even has to go to the jail.

A man should have the same attitude or mentality in honour and dishonour. He should not be too elated when he finds himself an honored person suddenly one day nor should he be dejected if disrespect comes his way. He should face everything knowing that everything is temporary. One should face everything with equanimity of mind.

There was a rich man in New York, a very rich man. Although he was rich he was not happy. He always felt that something was eluding him. He wanted to find true happiness. He heard about India and he understood that in the Himalayas there were Yogis who could clear his doubt. He sold his palatial mansion, gave away his riches and came to the Himalayas. He went to a great Yogi in the Himalayas and asked him where to find true happiness and what was the greatest thing to be known in life. The Yogi replied only four words and kept silent. He said, "This will also pass." So if something untoward has happened to you do not be crestfallen. This will also pass. If you are in a bad predicament, have hope, this will also pass. All the same if you are in a happy comfortable disposition be aware, this will also pass. Nothing is predictable. Quesara Sara, whatever will be will be the future is not our's to see, Quesara Sara. Anything might happen at any moment. The most fleeting thing is life, most ephimeral. So why be haughty or proud or be angry?

There is a wonderful story of what is most precious in life. There was a wood cutter who used to go to the forest daily and bring wood and sell it in town. One day as he was going to the forest he happened to find a Yogi sitting underneath a tree and meditating.He went to the Yogi and prostrated before him. The Yogi asked his purpose of coming to the forest which the woodcutter answered. Then the Yogi said, " You are a fool.You are going daily to a particular distance to the forest and bringing wood.If you go a little farther you can find something more precious." So the woodcutter went a little farther away inside the forest and to his wonder he found a bag of silver coins. He came back to his home after thanking the Yogi. A month passed when he exhausted his silver coins and he dredged the forest path to again cut wood. He again found the Yogi underneath the tree and the Yogi told him," you are a fool.If you go a little farther inside the forest you will get something more precious." So the woodcutter started walking and as he went farther inside the forest to his amazement he found a bag of gold coins. Happily he came home thanking the Yogi. But after two months the treasure was spent away and he again decided to go to the forest. As he went by the beaten path, he found the Yogi there and this time when he prostrated the Yogi told him," you are a fool. If you go inside farther interior to the forest you will find something more precious." So the woodcutter walked farther interior to the forest and to his joy he found a bag of diamonds. He retraced his steps and came to thank the Yogi when the Yogi told him, "You are a fool. You very well know that I knew where the silver, gold and diamonds were but you also know that I did'nt go hunting for them. So there must be something more precious that I might have found. You are a fool. Don't you want to know what that most precious thing in life is?" The woodcutter was only very eager to possess the most precious thing in life and so the Yogi told him to sit near him, close his eyes and meditate. Soon the woodcutter discovered the most precious thing in life. He realized himself.

There is a very important question that Arjuna asks Sri Krishna in *The Bhagavad Gita* Chapter 3 Sloka 36.

Atha kena prayuktoyam papam charathi purushah
Anichchannapi varshneya baladiva niyojitha.

Meaning: Oh! Krishna, why does man do sin even against his liking as if he is being compelled to do so?

Bahgawan Replies in Chapter 3 Sloka 37

Kamaesha krodha esha rajogunasamudbhava
Mahashano mahapapma vidyenamiha varinam.

Meaning: It is lust, it is anger which evolves out of Rajoguna which compels man to do sin. These are the two great enemies of men.

It destroys true knowledge and realization in man. Although man has his "free will" he deliberately commits acts which are not to his own liking. His "rajoguna" compels him to do the wrong. The best way to get out of this predicament is to dedicate whatever we do to God.

Man has three types of qualities, nature or gunas. The satwa guna or noble quality, the Rajoguna or activity impelling quality and the Thamoguna the sleep inducing or soporific quality. There is nothing in this universe which is not affected by these qualities. Every second we are bound to have one of these qualities.In the Hindu mythology the Trinity correspond to the three qualities. Lord Vishnu to Sattwa Guna-He is the protector, Prajapatji Brahma to Rajoguna-he is the creator and bhagawan Shiva to Thamoguna-He is the destroyer. It is told that Brahman is beyond these three qualities.

A lone traveller had to cross a dense forest. While in the middle of the forest three robbers caught hold of him. The first robber looted all his belongings and wanted to get rid of him but the second robber insisted that they tie him to a tree with a rope. So the traveller was in this hapless condition tied to the tree. After the robbers had departed the third robber felt pity for the traveller. He returned to where the traveller was tied, freed him and showed him the way out of the forest. The traveller requested the robber to accompany him to a wayside inn and treat himself to his hospitality but he refused and he departed.

The three Gunas are just like the robbers. The Thamoguna will loot you of all your worthy possessions and will want to get rid of you. The Rajo Guna will bind you to the world. The Sattwa Guna will free you from bondage and show you the way out but won't be a companion to you in your journey to the Supreme. You have to transcend all the gunas to realize the ultimate.

As a passing reference it can be pointed out that the three main pillars of the Indian democracy, the executive, the legislature and the judiciary can be compared to the Trinity. The Executive to Vishnu-the protector, the legislature to Brahma-the creator and the Judiciary to Shiva the destroyer. It is the play of all these three that takes place in this universe.

Chapter II

Time And Space

How much time does it take for one to experience a dream? One can experience a whole life time of a king or a beggar within a few seconds. As long as you were dreaming the dreamworld was real to us. The Atma is beyond time and space. Time and space are illusions created by our mind, as the world is only a projection of the mind. There is a story of a queen to illustrate this.A queen wanted to live happily with her king husband for a pretty long time.She knew death was unpredictable. So she did penance for a considerable period and propitiated Goddess Saraswathi. The Goddess was pleased with her austerities and gave her a boon that the King's soul wouldn't leave the palace when he died and that the Goddess would appear before her whenever she prayed to the Goddess. After sometime the king bade farewell to the world and the bereaved queen prayed to Goddess Saraswathi, who appeared before her. The Goddess told her to preserve the King's body in the palace itself bedecking it with flowers and told her the King's soul would remain in the palace itself.After some days the queen got disgusted.She felt lonely and bored and prayed to the Goddess who appeared. She wanted to know what had become of the King's soul.So Goddess Saraswathi asked her to close her eyes and in a trice they were in another world, in a palace where another king was ruling.As the queen watched from above, she was astounded to see that the King resembled her dear husband. In due course as they watched the King had to wage a war and was killed.Then Goddess Saraswathi took the queen to another world where the king was born again and he was living as an ordinary peasant. The Goddess explained to the queen that it was her husband itself who was born again as the King and the peasant. The soul can experience many births and deaths in numerous worlds within a specific time frame.Time and space are illusions.Atman is beyond time and space. The world is a projection of the mind.The jeevatma undergoes birth in various worlds as per the vasana or accumulated desires or samskaras of the mind. The sole purpose of a birth is to experience what mind has desired, to fulfil and extinguish the desire. But in the process mind cultivates new desires and the soul is reborn again and again.

I may be permitted to quote here a beautiful poem by Herbert Asquith.

Come and change, come and change
Into anything you will
Lion elephant or bear
Or a tropic bird with a painted bill;
Which creature of the earth or air
Sky and sea scale and fin, fur and hair
Which will you be?
Closer, closer draw you near one by one
I have but to lift my hand
And it is done!
Would you be swift as the gazelle?
Here is more than fancy dress
A slip of drappled loveliness
Streaking the shadows of a dell
Would you be a specked thrush,
A squirrel arching in a tree
A warbler on a waving rush?
Or turn into a honey bee

Paddling in gold to find his prize
And raising high his fairy halls
With the magic of a thousand walls:-
Or with a lark take wing and rise
To shimmer in the morning skies.

The soul may take any number of births till the vasanas or desires are exhausted.

The story of Gajendra the elephant king in Bhagavatham throws light on the fact that a being takes birth to complete a specific objective.No birth is wasted. There was a king named Indradyumna who was an ardent devotee of Lord Mahavishnu. Once, while he was doing penance on Malaya Hills, the Great Sage Agasthya visited him. Since the king was in meditation he was unaware that the sage had come and so he didn't do the customary respects to the sage. An enraged sage cursed the king that he be born as an elephant. When the king regained his consciousness his compatriots told him what had transpired. The king immediately went to the presence of Sage Agasthya and begged him to pardon him since he was doing penance when the sage visited him. The sage repented for his outburst but blessed the king saying he would continue to have devotion to the Lord even if he is born as an elephant. In due course Indradyumna was born as Gajendra, the elephant king. He roamed freely in the Trikuta Mountains with a retinue of she-elephants. He was the most powerful and the most majestic one born among elephants. One day when he had roamed for a pretty long time in the forests of Trikuta he felt exhausted and with his herd of elephants entered the lake named Rithumath in the valley of the mountain to drink the cool waters of the lake and quench his thirst.

There was celestial being named HUHU who, due to the curse of sage Devala, had been born as an alligator and was living in the lake. The alligator caught hold of the leg of Gajendra the elephant king. The elephant tried to get himself free from the jaws of the alligator by pulling with all his might and there was great tug of war between the alligator and the elephant. The elephant could not budge from his place. The Gajendra due to the blessings of sage Agasthya had not forgotten his devotion to the Lord to whom he used to offer flowers daily by plucking them with his trunk and mentally submitting it at the Lord's feet. Many days passed since the alligator had caught hold of its leg and Gajendra was getting weaker and his entire strength was waning. Still he persisted to offer the lotus flowers to the Lord praying ardently to Him and finally Lord heard his pathetic supplication. He came mounting on his vehicle Garuda, killed the alligator with the chakra or wheel weapon. Thus He gave freedom and salvation to the celestial being HUHU and he also gave salvation to the elephant king Gajendra. Thus both the elephant and the alligator were redeemed from their menial births. Paving the way for the purpose of their births to be fulfilled.

As there is a reason for every birth, the Hindu mythology narrates a story behind every special phenomenon in the earth. There is a story on how the sea water became salty and unfit to drink.

Once there was a very powerful asura or demon called Tharaka. He was causing much harm to the Devas and although the king of the Devas, Indra, fought with Tharaka he was defeated and was compelled to seek assistance of Brahma. Brahma advised him to make a weapon out of the spine of Maharshi Dadichi with which he could kill Tharaka. Dadichi Maharsi had acquired untold merit through his austerities and his bone would be so pure and powerful that it could kill the Asura. The Devas approached Maharshi Dadichi who was most sympathetic on hearing the plight of the

Devas and so he sacrificed himself for a great cause. Thus Indira made the powerful Thunder bolt weapon with the spine of Maharshi Dadichi and he attacked Tharaka and his forces. The mighty Tharaka was killed and his followers fled to far off places. They ran and ran and found shelter underneath the sea. The Devas couldn't penetrate to the bottom of the sea and the asuras started causing immence trouble by coming out of the sea at the dark hours of the night and creating havoc. The Devas sought the help of Brahma who advised them to go to Mahavishnu. Mahavishnu heard their cause and told them there was only one person who could solve their problem and that was sage Agasthya. The Devas went to sage Agastya and started singing his praises. The sage knew their need and started drinking the waters of the Ocean. By the time the Devas completed their prayers to sage Agastya he had drunk the entire waters of the Ocean and the Asuras had nowhere to hide and the Devas killed all of them. Now this was a sad predicament since the multitude of creatures in the ocean had to survive and Brahma requested sage Agastya to release the water. The sage informed that he had digested all the water and the entire quantity of it was in his urine form and he was pleased to release it back to the ocean. That is why the sea water is salty and undrinkable.

The soul discards one body and enters a new body as men discard old worn out clothes and adorn new ones. When the soul leaves one body it takes with it the samskaras or vasanas or desires as air takes with it the fragrance in a flower. When the soul is reborn in a new body it acts according to the accumulated vasanas or desires or samskaras, which is also called the accumulated karma.

These two slokas quoted here from *The Bhagavad Gita* are eye openers to the soul's destination, purpose and progress in life, when born.

Chapter 2 Sloka 22

Vasamsi jirnani yatha vihaya navani grhinnathi naroparani
Thatha sarirani vihaya jirnanyani samyathi navani dehi

Meaning: As a man casting off worn out garments puts on new ones, so the embodied soul casting of worn out bodies enters into others that are new.

Chapter15 Sloka 8

Shariram yadavapnothi yachhapyulkramatheeswaraha
Griheethvethani samyathi vayurgandhanivashayat

Meaning: When the Lord attains a body and when he leaves it, he takes these (the senses and the mind-the upadhis) and goes as the wind carries the scent from their sources.

The Sanchitha karma, the Prarabda Karma and the Aagami karma are the three types of Karma.The karmas cling to the soul as dirt in a mirror and it is to wipe away the karmas or dirt or polish the mirror that birth is taken on earth. To exhaust accumulated good karmas and bad karmas various types of people are born on earth.Not only people but the entire flora and fauna.This also explains how geniuses and extra ordinary men are born. One does karma to wipe away the bad karmas or vasanas and a Yagna is a sacrifice you do in the name of God or an action in God's name.Every action can be converted to a Yagna if it is done as an offering to God.

There was a Yogi who was staying near the house of an ill-reputed woman- a harlot. At the beginning he called her and advised her to abandon her profession and start a clean life. Her conscience was pricked but she had a weak mind and she continued to entertain men of base character. Each time she had the thought in her mind that she was doing something bad and in her helplessness she would beg the pardon of God. The Yogi who was watching her every move would take a pebble and throw it into a particular spot each time a man came to call on the lady. After a period of time there was a quite a huge heap of pebbles and one day the Yogi called the lady and showed her the heap. The lady repented from the bottom of her heart.It was sort of a shock to her and soon she bade goodbye to the world. The Yogi too in a short while expired and he was taken to hell.Before being taken to hell it is the practice to show the person what is heaven. When the Yogi reached heaven to his wonder he found the lady enjoying every comfort of heaven. This made him lose his temper and he accosted the God of death-Yama as to why this injustice was done to him. Yama replied that although the lady had a bad profession she had remembered God each time she indulged in her activity and she had also sincerely repented for her wrong doings which had absolved her of all her sins. On the other hand although the Yogi was supposed to be doing penance all his thoughts were in the harlot's activity. His mind was always in the harlot's house. His life had become futile. Bhagawan has declared in the Gita Chapter 9, Sloka 30 even though a man may be of most sinful conduct he may be considered righteous, a person of right resolve, if he had undeviated devotion to the Lord. It is the thoughts that make one good or bad.

There were two friends who were very close to each other.One evening they decided to go for a long walk. As they went past a temple they heard religious discourses on the Bhagavatham being conducted.One of the friends told the other that he wanted to listen to it but the other tried to persuade his friend to go to a harlot's house and enjoy the night. The first person did not agree and he went to the temple and although he was listening to the religious discourses till late hours, his mind was with his friend who had gone to the house of ill repute. He was repenting in his mind for not going with his friend. The other person who had gone to enjoy the night with the woman of ill repute couldn't enjoy the night at all. He was constantly thinking of his friend who was enjoying the nectar of the religious discourses and he repented for coming to this place and the colossal loss he had incurred. The Guru points out the second person who went to the house of ill repute was better in the eyes of Yama or God of death since his thought were centered on God all night. He had acquired better merit. It is thoughts that make a man.

 Sri Paramahansa Yogananda brings the concept of the thoughtrons to describe the thought waves. Every moment we are influenced by these thought waves or thoughtrons. Sometimes it might be good thoughts and at other times it might be bad. These thought waves induce us to do a deed. The prayers or Japa or Yagna we do is to ward off the evil thought entering the mind. One's mind radio is attuned to the good thought waves. By doing Japa or prayers regularly noble thoughts enter the mind. One is guided to the right path and one is guided to arrive at correct decisions in one's day to day life. Most importantly one is unknowingly restrained from committing sin.One might want to do something against one's conscience but something will control one's impulse to do the wrong act. One is also guided to buy the winning lottery ticket, to meet one's future beloved spouse, to the advertisement which will give one the most wanted break in one's life. It is not a joke. A sincere prayer gives one immense benefits.It is the strength in one's faith in a higher power and faith can move mountains.

How do miracles happen? It is faith, the belief that does it.Jesus before doing a miracle would ask the person whether he believed in The Father. The miracles happened-the sick were cured, the dumb man spoke, the deaf man heard, the lame man walked, the blind man's eyesight restored because they believed in the Heavenly Father.The Father was praised.

Chapter III

Arjuna And Sri Krishna

Arjuna and Sri Krishna can be described as the Jeevatma and Paramatma-The soul in man and the Supreme Lord. The Paramatma wants always to come to the rescue of the jeevatma whenever he is in difficulty provided he is devoted like Arjuna to Sri Krishna. On a number of occasions Krishna has saved the life of Arjuna. Most of the times subduing his pride. There is the story of Santhanagopalam where Krishna saved the honour and life of Arjuna by enabling him to bring the ten Brahmana children back from Vaikuntha-The abode of Vishnu, where Mahavishnu had hidden them in order to pave the way of meeting Arjuna and Krishna together. Arjuna who had promised the Brahmana to save his tenth child found himself in a spot when even the physical body of the child was not seen upon its birth although Arjuna had built a fortress like enclosure with his arrows where the child was to be born. When he was about to immolate himself after failing to find the child in the Yamaloka, nether regions and all other places the all knowing Krishna came to his rescue. There is another very interesting story of subduing Arjuna's pride and Krishna again came to his rescue.

It was after Arjuna had received the boon of using the Pashupathastra from none other than Lord Shiva, while he was coming down the Himalayas with a head full of pride that he met an old monkey on the way.On enquiry the monkey told him he was Hanuman-the son of wind God. Arjuna told him he was happy to meet such a great personage as Hanuman but wanted one of his doubts cleared. He asked Hanuman why Sri

Rama the greatest wielder of the bow and arrow had to seek the help of the monkey army in order to construct a bridge over the sea to cross over to Lanka. Why couldn't he construct the bridge with his arrows? Hanuman replied that although Sr Rama was a divine incarnation he did not want to demonstrate to the world his divinity by constructing the bridge with his arrows. He wanted to show the world that he was a normal human being. So he sought the help of the monkey army. Arjuna who was drunk with pride wanted to belittle Sri Rama and told Hanuman that he thought that Sri Rama did not know the art of building a bridge with arrows and that is why he did not carry out the endeavour. He told Hanuman strong and sturdy bridges could be built with arrows and in order to show off his prowess and ability he said he would construct a bridge over the pond which was nearby and Hanuman could walk and jump on it and cross over to the other side. Hanuman told him that any bridge he could construct would not withstand his strength and would break if Hanuman stepped on it. The arrogant Arjuna asserted that the bridge he constructed would never break and he took a vow that if the bridge collapsed he would immolate himself then and there. Hanuman in answer, told him he would present himself on top of Arjuna's flag staff of his chariot in the Kurukshetra war if the bridge did not give way. So they agreed and Arjuna soon construced the bridge over the pond with his arrows. Hanuman was told to cross over. He told Arjuna that he would only place his right foot on the bridge for fear that it would collapse and slowly placed his right foot on the bridge and Lo! The bridge collapsed. Arjuna was sorrow stricken. He repented for being too much proud. He had to keep his word and he started to bring wood from the nearby forest to make a pyre to immolate himself. Suddenly there appeared a strange Yogi in front of Hanuman and Arjuna. The Yogi asked Arjuna what he was upto and Arjuna told him what had transpired there. The Yogi after hearing everything told both of them that since there was no witness to their match it was not right that Arjuna immolate himself. Since now the Yogi was present as a witness Arjuna should construct the bridge again and Hanuman test its strength. So it was agreed and Arjuna again constructed the bridge across the pond. Hanuman slowly palced his right foot on the bridge but nothing happened. So he placed his left foot and then he started walking on the bridge but the bridge seemed strong enough to support him even when he started jumping in the middle.A visibly perturbed Hanuman surmised that something was amiss and so he looked underneath the bridge.He found that a giant tortoise was supporting the bridge on its back.He knew this was something extra-ordinary and as he turned and gazed at the Yogi he found Lord Sri Rama standing in the place of the Yogi.Arjuna too observed the tortoise under the bridge and as he stared at the Yogi he found Lord Krishna smiling and looking at him.Both of them came running and prostrated before the Yogi.Sri Krishna told Arjuna not to ridicule great personages and told him he himself was Sri Rama.He told Hanuman that since the Bridge did not collapse Hanuman had to fulfil his part of the deal and he had to be present on top of Arjuna's flag staff in the Kurukshetra war.Hanuman agreed and the trio bid farewell.

Everybody knows *The Bhagavad Gita* is the song celestial and it is a discourse by Sri Krishna to Arjuna. Here it is important to understand that while imparting *The Gita*, Krishna, the teacher was on a lower seat- that of the charioteer and Arjuna was on a higher seat that of the chariotman. It is peculiar to *The Gita*. Usually it is the teacher who is on a higher plane and the disciple on a lower seat. The chapters of the Gita are titled as Yogas.But why is the first chapter titled "Arjuna Vishada Yoga?" Is there a Yoga called Arjuna Vishada Yoga?

The answer can be interpreted in this way. Arjuna the great warrior finds himself in acute agony and distress when he finds his grandsire, teacher and close relatives on the opposite side of the battle field. The thought that he had to kill all these, his kinsmen, in order to win the war brings uncontrollable remorse and sadness in him.He says he is about to faint. He tells the Lord that he is unable to conclude what is right or wrong, whether to kill his kinsmen or not to battle and take recourse to Sanyasa. This dilemma is parching his senses. His understanding is confused as to what his duty is and he tells Krishna, "I fall at your feet, I am your disciple. Please instruct me on what I should do at this juncture." Now Vyasa Bhagawan is setting the tone for the most profound teachings in the form of the Song Celestial which will be beneficial to the whole world community. Before imparting true knowledge to his disciple an ideal Guru or teacher has to be convinced that his disciple is ready to accept the knowledge he is going to impart. Water cannot be held in an upside down vessel.It has to be ready to receive the contents and the Guru should know how much water can be poured into the vessel. Arjuna has lost all his vigour and pride. He is on bended knee before Krishna.It is sure that what Krishna is going to impart would percolate and sink down in Arjuna's mind. Here is a true disciple. The state of the mind is conducive to yoga and so the chapter is titled Arjuna Vishada Yoga. It is pertinent here that the state of Arjuna's mind in the first chapter is fully revealed in the beginning of the second chapter.

Although we find Arjuna in a state of inaction his mind in turmoil, he is in continuous action.This is what is inaction in action.Whereas when we take the case of Bhagawan Krishna, although he is driving the chariot and engaged in action, he exhibits total calmness. His mind is steady and unflickering i.e it is in inaction. This is what is action in inaction.Bahgawan Krishna says a wise man has to see action in inaction and inaction in action.

See *The Bhagavad Gita* Chapter 4 Sloka 18

Karmanyakarma yaha pahyeddakarmani cha karma yaha
Sa buddhiman manushyeshu sa yukthaha kritsnakarmakrit

Meaning: He who sees inaction in action, and action in inaction, he is wise among men, he is a yogi and accomplisher of everything.

Any athlete or sportsperson who is adept in his area of activity, would be like Krishna in the chariot of Arjuna. Take for instance Pete Sampras or Roger Federer; even if they are playing the most terrific contest their mind will be calm and their face will radiate coolness and peace. I remember one instance when Harsha Bhogle was interviewing Sachin Tendulkar, he was asked what was going on in his thought process while he was batting and scoring centuries.Sachin replied that his thought process stopped at that period of time, he was not thinking of anything. Only his bat was doing the talking. This is action in inaction.If you want to attain a superlative stage in any enterprise your mind has to reach that state like the mind of the Zen master- calm and peaceful. In ideal meditation all action is completely stopped of both the mind and the body. It is absolute actionless state.

Sri Krishna was the true Guru and companion to Arjuna and he gave away his sister Subhadra in wedlock to Arjuna although there was opposition from his brother Balarama. Arjuna is indebted to Krishna in all ways.

Sri Ramakrishna Paramahamsa says the human beings are zeroes. Sri Krishna Paramatma is the number one.The zeroes have no value.But if the number one is put in front of the zeroes then it gets value.So we have to always place God or Paramatma in front of us.Then whatever we do will have value.It is the practice everywhere when starting a new venture or when you start staying in a new house or, for that matter for any important thing in your life, you first worship God Almighty. Otherwise we believe the venture will not be successful.This is putting in number one before the zeroes.

Arjuna and Krishna can be taken as the example of the two birds perched on the branches of the same tree. The one, which is on the higher branch, doesn't do anything.It just sits there basking in its glory. The other bird, which is in the lower branch, enjoys the sweet and sour fruits of the tree.As the different tastes stings it, .it looks up at the other bird and wants to become like him — peaceful and calm.Slowly he climbs himself to the side of the other bird higher and higher.When he reaches there he finds that there are no two birds, it was his own image.It is the same case with the jeevatma and paramatma.They are the two birds.The body is the tree.The jeevatma partakes of the happiness and sorrow in the world experienced through the body and at times he looks up and sees the image of the Paramatma. He strives to go up and up and wants to become like the paramatma. When he finally reaches the Zenith he finds that he himself is the Paramatma and merges in Him. Arjuna and Krishna are the same.

Chapter IV

Love Thy Neighbour

"Love Thy Neighbour as thyself" is an oft quoted biblical saying.It says you love your neighbour as you love yourself. If you want to love a person, the person should be understandably pure in character. Which means you wouldn't like to love a person who is bad tempered, who barks at you, who is always criticising you. The same way with yourself. If you want to love yourself you should be free from bad temper, free from malice, free from all bad qualities. Then only you will love thyself. Then you can love your neighbour as you love thyself. If you are a man with 80% bad qualities you will love thyself only 20% and you will love thy neighbour only 20% so the solution to the problem is to make yourself a better person. The more you love thyself the more light is shed on you and in turn you will love your neighbour more. Love is something boundless. A neighbour is a person who is near to you. It could be your wife, children or your parents. The best way to practice loving thy neighbour is by loving your wife and then your children and your parents. Love should evolve in the family among the close knit family members. The best way to show your love is to speak out your love.You should tell your wife "I love you dear wife" or to your son and parents "I love you dear son or parents." Love is something which should be expressed. We keep our love inside us and we are reluctant or afraid or shy to express it. It is like storing valuable and treasures in a locker. Nobody sees it, it is of no use to anybody. You exhibit it at rare occasions just to show off your treasure. Love should not be like that. Express it and you will find a tremendous change in the family atmosphere for the good.

Chapter 7 Sloka 7 in *The Gita* is very significant. It says:

Matthhaha paratharam nanyat kinchidasthi
Dhanajaya
Mayi sravamidam protham suthre manigana eva

Meaning: There is nothing whatsoever higher than Me, Oh, Dhananjaya, All these are strung on me as rows of gems on a string.

The string that connects everything is the string of love. All the beings are compared to gems. Every creature is precious to the Lord. Love is the summum Bonum in everything. Where do we start to find that love?

A man accidentally found a very costly piece of gold studded gem.He dug a hole in the outside of his garden and hid the gem inside the hole. Everyday after midnight he would get out of his bed sneak to the garden and inspect whether the gem was there. One day one of his servants happened to see what he was upto. The servant, without the man's knowledge, stole the gem. Next day when the man came to inspect the gem he found that it had been stollen. He became sad and remorse.An old friend of his, who came to know about the incident, advised him to place a small stone in place of the gem in the hole and pretend that it was the gem and inspect it daily as before. He explained that it was all the same since the gem was of no use to him and he only looked at it daily. This is one of Aesop's fables and I want to point out here that our love should not be like the man's gem.

When you go out on a tour always you should bring something for your loved ones. You might not be able to afford a costly gift but even a small flower given with true love can make a world of difference. Even if you truly don't love a person the expression of love by words or gift would change the other person's whole picture about you. Try it once and it will do wonders. Start with your wife. Almost all the problems today in a household, the increasing number of cases of divorce, is due to the lack of expressing your love.

Even Kuchela who was almost a beggar found it appropriate to carry a handful of parched rice to offer it to his good old friend Krishna tied in a rag when he went to visit him. His wife who had secured a handful of rice begging from the nearby households pounded the rice and with utmost love told Kuchela to offer it to the Lord. And what did the Lord give him in return? The Lord blessed him with immense wealth, a palatial mansion and a number of servants. Kuchela had felt ashamed to place the rag of rice before Krishna and the Lord had to snatch it from his armpit.

The mantra to foster a happy and peaceful family life is that there should be no "ego" problem between the husband and wife. The attitude should be,"Even if we do not have much, we have each other." One should be content with what one has. There should always be mutual respect and love among the partners. One should have the mind to appreciate even small small things that the partner does. See only the good. One should love "in spite of" the partner's short comings. That is true love.

Which is the greatest love in this world? You might say it is the love of the mother for her child. The mother is very much concerned for the child indeed. She is even prepared to sacrifice herself for the sake of the child. A guru's love for his shishya or disciple is ideal. Guru is one who removes darkness and brings light into one's mind. He is the embodiment of love. How does a true Guru take care of his Chela or disciple? There is a beautiful story to illustrate this. There was a man who went to his Guru and told him he had decided to marry, to find a partner for his life. The Guru asked him whether he was firm in his resolve. He replied in the affirmative. But that night the man had an insatiable urge to visit the house of a lowly woman and enjoy her company. He went walking to her house and at the gate he found a guard who told him the woman was busy dressing herself up and asked him to come a little while later. The man went away and returned to her house after a couple of hours and this time the gate keeper told him she was having guests and she was not to be disturbed. The man went back a bit sad and again at dawn he returned to the house to find the gate keeper telling him she had retired to her rooms and was not entertaining anybody that day any more. The visibly depressed man went to his Guru in the early morning hours to confess his fickle mindedness but he found that his Guru was sound asleep. He was astonished to note this since it was brahma muhurtha, the most auspicious hour of the day, and the Guru never defaulted to observe his austerities like meditation and prayer at this time. He awoke the Guru who told him all night he was guarding his Shishya or disciple from going to the house of ill repute and indulge in immoral activities and so he had not slept the whole night.

A true Guru intuits your future, past and present. Not only that he can tell you everything about your past incarnations and when your soul will be ready for salvation, after how many more births.

See Sloka 61 in Chapter 18 of *The Bhagavad Gita* where Bhagawan says:

Easwara sarvabhuthanam hriddheshe Arjuna
thishtathi
Bhramayan sarvabhuthani yandrarudhani mayaya

Meaning: The Lord dwells in the heart of all beings, Oh, Arjuna, and by His maya causes all beings to revolve as though mounted on a machine.

So one's self is the Lord Himself. But the greatest love a man has is for his own self. He commits sin, he gets angry, he gets jealousy, he gets lust all for his own self. Why is a man greedy? Because he has the true self in him which is the Lord of the universe. Everything in this universe is his and the poor man, when he sees something precious, is a prey to self aggrandizement. He wants to possess it, he wants to enjoy it. He wants to realize that everything is his. He wants to realize that self.What is desire for carnal pleasure? It is the persistant attempt or work one does to enjoy what one desired for. Self is the most beautiful thing. Most beautiful.Hence the craving to enjoy the beauty or bliss when one sees beauty in another.It is his own self. That is why one goes wandering from one beautiful thing to the other to find, to experience the bliss, the ecstasy. After enjoying one he thinks he will get more bliss from the other so he goes on from one thing to the other. And beauty lies in the eyes of the beholder.One thing which might be ugly to me might be beautiful for the other. It is the senses that make you go astray.

The body is the chariot, the senses are the five horses and the mind is the rein. Your destination is the Supreme.Your atma or jeevatma is the one who is sitting in the chariot like Arjuna. We must make Krishna the God as the charioteer. Always make His will as our will. Otherwise everything will go astray. The mind, the reins will have no control over the horses or senses and man will be facing one difficulty after the other.

Swami RamaThirtha narrates the story of the horse and the rider. It is the practice in India to distribute sweets when some auspicious thing takes place. There was this man who was distributing delicious sweets to everybody that he met. When asked what was the joyous occasion to celebrate, he told he had lost his horse. Everybody was making fun of him. Then he revealed the secret that although the horse was lost the rider had been saved. It was a great thing, we are all concerned with the horse-the body always. We are trying to save the horse or the body every moment. We are not bothered about the rider, the self or the soul.It is to save the soul that we should strive. We are getting angry, envy, jealousy hatred and what not for the body.We accumulate wealth to pamper the body. We are not concerned what happens to the soul. We should realize that this soul or the self is something other than the body and that it never perishes even if the body mutilates. It is that which never can be destroyed and the essence of everything in this universe.It is permeating the whole universe from the finite to the infinite. There is an interesting story in the Chandogyopanishad of how a father makes his son understand what is this essence that is pervading the existence of everything in this universe.

Udhalaka the son of Aruni was a great sage. He, through his study of the scriptures and severe austerities, had realized the Supreme. His name and fame had spread all over the country side. He had a son named Swathakethu who was least interested in acquiring knowledge.His main occupation in his childhood was to play with his friends all the time and to fill his stomach when he was hungry. Udhalaka was very much perturbed about the way his son was growing up.So one day he called him to his side and told him he was born in a family of great ascetics and scholars and he should not while away his time in worthless pursuits but must study well under an able Guru, a preceptor and become a pride of his family. Swathakethu reluctantly agreed to be admitted to a

Gurukula or Hermitage school. There he studied *The Vedas*, scriptures and grammar for a number of years. After completion of his studies he returned to his father's house one day. Swathakethu was very proud of his knowledge and was haughty in his behaviour. One look at him and Udhalaka knew his son had not grasped the essence of all learning. A true student of the Vedas and one who has mastered the Vedas must be an embodiment of humility. So Udhalaka called his son one day to his side and asked him, "Son, Have you studied the Vedas and scriptures thoroughly to the extent that you have no doubts in your mind?" Swathakethu replied in the affirmative. Then Udhalaka told his son, "If you have correctly understood the scriptures, tell me, son, by which is that when you have seen you don't have to see anything more, by which is that when you have heard you don't have to hear anything more and by which is that when you have known, you don't have to know anything more?" Swathakethu was perplexed and he recollected all he had studied but he stood dumbfounded not answering. So Udhalaka explained to him again, "There are so many substances and things on this earth. Even in numerous births one cannot study the essence of all these substances one by one. Just as from gold various ornaments are made and different names are given to these ornaments but the main ingredient in all these ornaments is gold. So if you know gold you know the essence of all these ornaments. Now son, you answer my question."

A stupefied Swathakethu told his father that his Guru had not taught him all these. His pride was shattered and he begged his father to tell him the answer.Udhalaka then explained to his son the birth of the universe right from the Supreme Paramatma or being.The Supreme being evolved this unverse from his conceptualisation. The five elements were produced water, ether, earth fire and wind. Then the

Supreme being manifested himself as the soul in all beings. It is called the *Jeevatma*. This jeevatma is the enlightened essence of all beings.If you know him you know everything. Nothing else need to be known.

Swathakethu had umpteen number of doubts in his mind and he asked his father how from one single being all these innumerable forms could manifest. By way of answer Udhalaka told his son to come to him after fifteen days but during the fifteen days he should completely fast. He can have only water.After fifteen days Swathakethu approached his father.Udhalaka asked him to recite the Vedas which he was unable to do.He couldn't recollect anything. Then Udhalaka asked his son to go and have food and when he had regained his stamina and health to come back to him.Accordingly Swathakethu when he regained his lost energy approached his father.When asked to recite the Vedas Swathakethu could recollect and recite them easily. So his father questioned as to why he was not able to recite the Vedas when he had undergone the fast.Swathakethu couldn't reply.Udhalaka explained to him in detail that this body is produced from food.Food is produced from water. The essence of water evolves from the splendour or brilliance of fire. This brilliance of fire, this spirit is none other than the individual soul or jeevatma. Mind gets its energy from food. Mind cannot function without depending on food.If food is not supplied mind becomes weak.When mind becomes weak your knowledge becomes veiled. You are not able to exhibit your knowledge.When the body is supplied with food, when it is in good health the intellect and mind function smoothly. The essence of all knowledge is the spirit or soul.When you know this soul or self you have attained supreme knowledge.You don't have to know anything else. When one realizes his self he attains bliss. That self is in you."Swathakethu, THOU ART THAT.

Udhalaka cleared his son's numerous doubts about the individual soul and the Supreme soul.With the example of how from a tiny small seed a huge tree is born Udhalaka explained that the universe is born likewise. Then Swathakethu had a doubt, how this self can be known, why it is not seen? Udhalaka asked him to put some salt in a basin of water. Then he asked his son where the salt had disappeared. Swathakethu said he did not know. Udhalaka asked him to taste the water and he said it is saltish.He asked him to taste the water in various parts of the vessel and Swathakethu said everywhere it tasted saltish. Udhalaka explained that in the same way as the salt in the water cannot be seen the self permeates in each part of the body and it cannot be seen. It can be realized through various means. A Guru or preceptor will show you the way to realize your Self. For one who realizes his Self there is no sorrow anymore.

Chapter V

Prayer, And How It Helps

I am reminded of a song "Teach Me How to Pray" which was one of my favourites.In that, a son one day asks his Daddy, " Daddy, you taught me how to throw the ball so high,you taught me lots today,but daddy,My daddy teach me how to pray." The father stands aghast. Tears well out of his eyes. He had not prayed for such long time, and he had forgotten how to pray. He didn't know what to tell his son.

 What is a prayer? A true prayer is a thanks giving to a higher power. You pray for the good health for the well being of your wife, father, mother, son, or daughter. If you are not praying at least for this, then, it means you do not love your dear ones. Why pray at all? If you deeply believe there is a higher power which is guiding you, which is sustaining you, which is protecting you, then there is a need for prayer. See the sun which rises daily without fail, and gives you sunlight and is the cause for the sustenance of the world. At least say a thanks to the sun for showering these precious rays on you.One should not be thankless. Your prayer never goes in vain. The only criterion is it should be sincere, from the heart. In *The Mahabharatha* we have two instances where Panchali the wife of the Pandavas prayed to Lord Krishna to come and rescue her.The Lord never disappointed her. He heard her heart felt appeal and provided succour.

First instance was when Dushasana dragged Draupadi (Panchali) by pulling her hair to Dhuryodana's assembly and tried to disrobe her. Her five valiant husbands were helpless witnesses to the brutal act.They were powerless to do anything.Panchali entreated to the Lord, to Lord Krishna to save her and guard her honour. The Lord heard her pathetic supplication and provided countless yards of her robe. Dushasana was unable to disrobe her completely and thoroughly exhausted, abandoned his attempt.

The second time was when the pandavas were staying in the forest after having lost their kingdom in gambling. The Sungod had blessed Dharma putra (Yudhishtira) with the "Akshayapatra"-a vessel which provides sumptuous food to all his retinue and it never exhausted till Panchali partook of her food. So it was the custom that Panchali always had her food in the end, after all stomachs were filled. The Kauravas knew the secret of the vessel and when sage Durvasa visited them Dhuryodhana tactfully sent him and his assemblage to the Pandavas at an untimely hour to have their food. There was no food left in the Pandava camp when sage Durvasa arrived since Panchali had eaten her meal. Dharmaputra requested the sage to have his ablutions in the nearby river. Panchali was upset to the core. She had to provide food otherwise the sage who was anger personified would curse them.In utter desperation she cried out to Lord Krishna from the bottom of her heart to come and save her. The Lord arrived there from nowhere and was visibly very hungry. He asked Panchali to give him something to eat. Panchali asked the Lord not to mock her since he knew that there was no food left in the Akshayapatra. The Lord requested her to search thoroughly inside the vessel, to see whether there was anything left. Panchali with no hope searched the vessel and found only one leaf of green leaf which she had served that day. The Lord asked her to bring it to him with a pitcher of water. He swallowed the leaf and emptied the pitcher of water into his mouth.His hunger seemed to have assuaged. Durvasa who had completed his bath felt that his stomach was completely full and it would burst if he ate anything more. With his divine powers he surmised what had happened. He told Dharmaputra that his hunger had been appeased without even eating anything, blessed him and departed. A heartfelt prayer has its results.

In *The Bhagavad Gita* Lord Krishna says four types of people pray to Him.Chapter 7, Sloka 16:

Chathurvdha bhajanthe mam Janah sukritinorjuna
Artho jijnasurartharthi, Gnani cha Bharatharishabha

Meaning: Four types of men worship me O! Arjuna. The man in distress, the man seeking knowledge, the man seeking wealth and the man imbued with wisdom.

These four types of people are in four stages of spiritual development. The man in distress seeks ways and means to come out of his predicament. He acquires knowledge.He continues worship and when he acquires knowledge wealth will find its way to him with the blessing of the Lord. When he is endowed with wealth and is steadfast in his worship he becomes detached to the world and soon is imbued with wisdom.The man of wisdom is the dearest to the Lord. A karmayogi who renounces the fruits of action, who does all enterprises as an offering to the Lord also reaches the Supreme state as that of the Gnani or man of wisdom.You will be amazed when you read this story of what great thinkers, scientists and men of action can do to this world and the worlds beyond with their perseverance and indefatigable spirit. Although it is a story that was told by Swami RamaThirtha in one of his speeches, it is an eye opener.

There was this Christian priest who had a doubt whether great thinkers and scientists like Aldous Huxley and Charles Darwin had gone to heaven or hell after their death. They were great men on earth and had done good work here, but they were not people who were completely devoted to the Bible or the Christian cause and so he concluded that they might have been deported to the lowest hell.Thinking thus he fell asleep and he had a strange dream. He dreamt that he had died and had gone to the gates of heaven. The guard there heard his cause and reluctantly permitted him to enter heaven. Now the priest asked the guard where Darwin and Huxley had been taken to and he was told they were in the lowest hell. His assumption was correct.He thought he would visit the lowest hell and preach the Bible to these people and convert them. So he asked permission from the guard to go to the lowest hell. After much consultation and deliberation the priest was permitted to go to the lowest hell. He boarded the train to go to the lowest hell. As the train was going down and down the atmosphere of the places was getting worse and by the time he reached one station prior to hell there was rotten smell and most pungent gaseous vapour was in the air. The stench was so unbearable that he had to cover his eyes and nose with towels he could lay hands upon but that didn't stop him from vomitting twice. At last when he reached the lowest hell he couldn't believe his eyes since the place was so tidy and clean and enchanting fragrance of newly blossomed flowers was emanating from the place. He had to ask a porter there twice whether he was indeed in lowest hell. He walked out of the station and he could see beautiful gardens and well kept lawns and the wonderful scent of flowers was again creeping into his nostrils. He walked steadily and he found a tall gentleman walking in front of him.He recollected seeing him somewhere, yes, the man was none other than Aldous Huxley. He greeted him and told him he could not believe that he was in the Lowest Hell. Mr.Huxley told him when he and Darwin arrived there it was in a horrible condition with steaming hot iron pits,dirty ditches of water and foul smelling dung etc.But when they were thrown into the dirty ditch they splashed the water with all their might and managed to pour and sprinkle some water in the hot iron pits. By the time they were put in the iron pits some of it had become cold and deftly manipulating the iron, they were able to make some implements, tools and machines. They put the dung from the pit to the soil pit with the implements and it became manure and soon they were able to grow plants and with the help of machines they were able to change the entire region into a heavenly abode. The story might be a dream story but there is lot of moral substance in it. When you do such a wonderful act as this it is a prayer. It is something good you are doing without expecting anything in return. Only for the good of the world. No prayer you chant, no prayer you recite goes in vain.It creates that much positive energy in the world. You should not think that it is insignificant. When the monkeys were constructing the bridge to cross over to Lanka, the tiny squirrels wanted to do something for Lord Rama. So they dipped themselves in the seawater and started rolling in the sand so that the sand particles would stick on to their body. They would run to the top of the bridge and shake off the sand from their body there so that the bridge would become strong. They tirelessly did this service to the Lord.Lord Rama was so much pleased that he lovingly caressed the back of the squirrels with his three fingers and it is believed those are the three lines that we still see on the squirrel's back.There is proverb in Malayalam which says, "every squirrel to his might" when you chant a prayer sincerely believe that you are doing something for the good of the world. That should be the idea or motto of living in the world, to do something good for your fellow being. You might not be able to donate lakhs of rupees for a worthy cause but this much you can do sitting in the comfort of your houses. Saying a few prayers for the benefit of the world.That will make you a worthy citizen of the world. Say a prayer for those who are less fortunate than you. Have a concern for them. Above all, believe that your prayer can make a change, a better world.

There was a farmer who had about 600 acres of coconut farm. He was very stingy and used to mint money by selling his coconuts periodically. When he became very old he was in his death bed. The doctor was summoned who advised his son to give him tender coconut water. Accordingly his son gave him tender coconut water and the man, after drinking the water, exclaimed, "This is so sweet! What a fool I am. I didn't know this was so sweet. Even though I was dealing in thousands of coconuts I didn't have the heart to taste even one tender coconut. I was so stingy."We must not be like that farmer.We have countless acres of coconut farms in the form of spiritual literature and if we do not enjoy the nectar like the water of the tender coconut in the form of *The Quran, The Bible,* and *The Bhagavad Gita* and other religious scriptures we will regret in our death bed. We should make it a point to study some of the scriptures. After all it was great men, the sages who revealed them. We are all fools if we don't drink that nectar.

In *The Bhagavad Gita* the Dhyana sloka compares all the Upanishads to a cow. Sri Krishna, the cowherd boy, is the man who milks the cow. Arjuna is the calf. Men of purified intellect are the drinkers of the milk of the cow which is the supreme nectar of the Gita.

Heaven and hell are all of our own making. This story illustrates this point. It is the way which with we deal with a problem that matters. When Mr.Nehru expired Moses came to take him away. On asking whether he wanted to go to heaven or hell he said that first he wanted to see both the places.He was taken to hell first where he saw that a big cauldron of soup was boiling.

All the people there were very much hungry and famished.They were making loud noises and fighting with each other. And there was utter chaos and pandamonium. On observing minutely Mr. Nehru saw that all the people were provided with individual spoons to drink the soup but the handles of the spoon was very very long and the soup wouldn't enter their mouths. So there was utter confusion. Then Mr.Nehru was taken to heaven. There he witnessed that the same cauldron of boiling soup and the same long handled spoons were provided to the people there but everything was calm and peaceful. It was a happy and joyous atmosphere. The reason being that the people were feeding each other. So it is we ourselves who make unrest or peace. It is all our attitude. We can make heaven out of hell provided we have a mind for it.

Chapter VI

Rambhakt Hanuman

Among the noteworthy characters of the Indian epics Hanuman holds an exemplary position. His service to Lord Rama was unparalleled. He is the connecting bond between the jeevatma and Paramatma, i.e the individual soul and the supreme spirit. Sita is the personification of the jeevatma in the Ramayana. When she is abducted by the evil minded Ravana and is imprisoned under the Simsupa tree in Lanka it was Hanuman as an emissary of Sri Rama who managed to find her in Lanka and paved the way for her reunion with the Lord. It is so with us human beings. When we are abducted by the evil thoughts and are in the grip of evil tendencies the Supreme Lord prompts us to reminisce a personage like Hanuman and soon we are freed from the evil entanglement. The Lord is so compassionate that he is always ready to help us. We in our ignorance and waywardness do not comprehend His helping hand.

There was this man who was walking on the seashore of life hand in hand with the Lord. Their footsteps made imprints on the sand beach. As the man reviewed the images of the footsteps he found that the Lord's footsteps were close by to his.i.e four footsteps side by side. As he advanced at a certain place he found only two footsteps on the sand. Then he remembered he was fatigued and very much tired at that time and was about to stumble and fall. He asked the Lord why the Lord had forsaken him and gone away when that was the time he needed his help very badly. The Lord replied He was carrying him on his back when he was in that state and the two footsteps were the Lord's. So he is there always beside you.We forget His presence.

How many of us know that Hanuman had a son? It was when the monkey army was in Lanka and was marauding the rakshasa forces that Ravana found himself in a very helpless predicament. He had lost Indrajith and Kumbhakarna in the battle and he was thinking deeply who would assist him in killing Rama and Lakshmana. Then he remembered his friend Ahi Ravana who was the king of the Nether Regions.So Ravana mounted his chariot and went to the Nether Regions. Ahi Ravana was pleased to receive him and Ravana told him the sad state of affairs in his camp and besought AhiRavana's help in destroying Rama and Lakshmana.Ahi Ravana, who was an adept in magic, consoled Ravana and told him that Rama and Lakshmana would be killed by him by foul or fair means without much delay. A visibly relieved Ravana left the Nether Regions glad at heart.

That night Ahi Ravana stealthily approached the monkey army camp with the idea of abducting Rama and Lakshmana somehow or other. But he found that Hanuman had made a fortress around the army camp with his tail and it was impossible to penetrate the camp. The shrewd Ahi Ravana thought for a while and by his magic powers he transformed himself in the perfect form of Vibhishna. He approached Hanuman and told him that he, Vibhishana, had gone to the seashore for meditation and Hanuman should lift his tail so that he could go to his camp. Hanuman was duped and Ahi Ravana entered the monkey camp.He stealthily went to the camp of Rama and Lakshmana who were in deep slumber, managed to gag them and tie them and with his magic powers make a tunnel and reach his palace in the Nether Regions. Pandamonium broke out in the monkey army camp when in the morning Rama and Lakshmana where seen nowhere.

The monkeys searched every nook and corner but their attempt to find the brothers ended futile. Hanuman then remembered that Vibhishana had gone out to the seashore in the night and he asked him whether he had seen Rama and Lakshmana anywhere near the shore. Vibhishana was emphatic that he had not gone anywhere in the night and so it was found out that somebody had disguised as Vibhishana and entered the monkey camp and abducted Rama and lakshmana.After much intense thought Vibhishana concluded that the culprit could be only Ahi Ravana. Hanuman immediately promised that he would himself go to the Nether Regions and search for the brothers and bring them back.But when he entered the Nether Regions and went to the gates of Ahi Ravana's palace he was wonderstruck to find a young monkey exactly like him guarding the entrance to the gates. On enquiry the young monkey replied that he was the son of Hanuman and his name was Makaradwaja. Hanuman told Makaradwaja that he was Nthyabrahmachari, a born ascetic who had not married and he never could have a son. Makaradwaja told Hanuman that once the sage Narada happened to meet him and told him about his antecedents. It seems when Hanuman was jumping over the sea to cross over to Lanka one drop of his perspiration fell into the sea and a shark swallowed the drop of sweat and it conceived a monkey child in its womb. A fisherman had caught hold of the shark and presented it to AhiRavana. When the fish was cut open the monkey child came out of its stomach and it grew up in the palace of Ahi ravana. He became as strong as Hanuman and the king made him the guardian of the entrance to the palace. On knowing that it was Hanuman himself who had come to find Rama and lakshmana Makaradwaja prostrated before his father who embraced him lovingly. On Hanuman's request to give way for him to the palace Makaradwaja emphatically refused permission saying he must be true to his king whose salt he had eaten. He also informed Hanuman he will have to defeat him in a fight if he wanted to enter the palace. So a great fight ensued between Hanuman and Makaradwaja at the end of which Hanuman overpowered Makaradwaja and tied him firmly with ropes and left him unconscious at the entrance. Hanuman immediately rushed inside the palace, searched every nook and corner and at last found Rama and Lakshmana securely tied to the pillars of the Kali temple. The statue of Kali was very huge and as he started hearing the sound of beatings of drum and beagles he hid behind the statue of Kalimatha. Soon Ahi Ravana entered with a large retinue of servants who were carrying large quantities of fruits and flowers in trays and baskets. Ahi Ravana prostrated before the statue of Kali and offered the fruits and flowers and as he closed his eyes and prayed Hanuman snatched the fruits from behind the statue and ate them. Ahi Ravana as he opened his eyes saw that the fruits had vanished and he thought that Mother Kali was pleased with his devotion and he loudly proclaimed to Mother Kali that he was going to sacrifice two human beings to please her more. Then Rama and Lakshamna were marched to the front of the statue and as Ahi Ravana raised his sword to behead them, Hanuman made a giant leap from behind the statue and gave a mighty blow with his mace on Ahi Ravana's head. The demon was killed in no time. Hanuman released Rama and Lakshmana who were extremely happy and they embraced him. Hanuman lifted them on his shoulders and as they were passing the gates of the palace Rama saw a second Hanuman tied to the pillars of the gate and was dumbfounded. When asked who the monkey was, Hanuman replied that he was his son Makaradwaja and narrated the story behind his birth and upbringing. Sri Rama told Hanuman to release Makaradwaja who sought the protection of the Lord. Sri Rama installed him the king of the Nether Regions.

The joyous monkey army celebrated the return of the princes.

In another strange story we have Hanuman and Rama confronting each other. Narada was instrumental in bringing about this confrontation. It was during Sri Rama's coronation, after killing Ravana, and returning victorious to Ayodhya with Sita. All the kings were invited to the coronation ceremony and they were all making haste to Ayodhya. As the Raja of Kasi was approaching Ayodhya, he was stopped in the way by no less a personage than Narada. Narada told Kasi Raja who made obeisance to him that he was to act in Sri Rama's coronation as Narada wanted him to do. Kasi Raja agreed and Narada told him that while entering the assembly of Rama he should not do obeisance to sage Vishwamitra alone. He should respect all others. A visibly perturbed Kasi Raja retorted that he would be turned to ashes by Viswamitra if he did not pay respects to him. Narada threatened that he himself would turn him into ashes if he did not do what he was told. Kasi Raja was in between the frying pan and fire and he reluctantly agreed. As directed by Narada when he entered the assembly he made obeisance to all the revered guests there but Vishwamitra. The sage was seething in anger and after the coronation when the sage met Sri Rama in his chambers Sri Rama intuited that Viwshwamitra had something disturbing in his mind which his face revealed. Although initially the sage was reluctant to divulge the matter. On persistent questioning, the sage told that he was very much aggrieved that in the assembly of the honoured guests Kasi Raja alone did disrespect to him by not doing the customary obeisance to him. Sri Rama got enraged when he knew the incident and he made a solemn vow then and there that by next night fall he would kill Kasi Raja with his arrow. The news spread and Kasi Raja started running away from Ayodhya. On the way Narada met him and an angry Raja rebuked him for his ill advice which led him to be killed by Sri Rama the next day. Narada consoled him and told him to board his veena which would take them to Kanchangiri in the Himalayas where Hanuman's mother Anjana was residing.He told Kasi Raja he should fall at the feet of Anjana and cling on to her feet till she promised to protect his life.They reached Kanchangiri and Kasi Raja ran to the presence of Anjana, fell at her feet and started wailing saying, "Mother, please protect me." Although Anjana tried to lift him up he wouldn't get up from her feet and Anjana had to promise that she would protect him from any harm. The relieved Kasi Raja got up from Anjana's feet and told her the entire incident that had happened. And that he was to be killed by Rama's arrows the next day. Now Anjana was in a very big dilemma and she stood there not knowing what to do but at that nick of time Hanuman came there to see his mother and do respects to her. Anjana made Hanuman promise that he would accomplish whatever his mother wanted his son to do. Then she told Hanuman that he was to save the life of Kasi Raja from Sri Rama's arrows. Hanuman was in a fix. He thought deeply for a long while, prostrated before his mother and bade good bye to her. He told Kasi Raja to ascend his shoulders and within minutes they traversed the distance form Kanchangiri to Ayodhya. When they reached the banks of the Sarayu River Hanuman told Kasi Raja to descend from his shoulders. He asked him to stand waist deep in the water and go on chanting Rama Nama loudly without any break till he met Sri Rama and returned. Kasi Raja did as he was told. Hanuman went straight to Sri Rama's presence and prostrated before the Lord. The Lord surmised that something was in Hanuman's mind and asked him to reveal it. Hanuman told Rama that he only wanted the Lord to remember his promise that he would safeguard the life of all his Bhakthas. He would not do any harm to them. On receiving the affirmation that he would protect all his bhakthas and that his promise would never go in vain Hanuman returned to the banks of the Sarayu where Kasi Raja was standing and chanting Rama Nama. While it was time for Sri Rama to fulfill his promise to Vishwamitra, he with the sage arrived at the banks of the Sarayu river.He found Kasi Raja in the water chanting the Rama nama and Hanuman standing on the river bank chanting Rama nama.Sri Rama was in a fix and when Vishwamitra urged Sri Rama to send the arrow at Kasi Raja he told him that it would be in vain. On persistant request from the sage Sri Rama sent an arrow towards Kasi Raja but the arrow went around his body and came and fell in Sri Rama's quiver without doing him any harm.Vishwamitra was enraged and he commanded Sri Rama to again send the arrow but again the arrow circumambulated Kasi Raja and fell in Rama's quiver. Just then Sage Vasishta arrived there and gauging the gravity of the situation he exhorted Hanuman to withdraw his protection of Kasi Raja so that Sri Rama could fulfil his vow. Hanuman replied that Kasi Raja was an ardent devotee of Sri Rama and he would not restrain himself from protecting any devotee of Sri Rama. Then Vasishta addressed Vishwamitra and asked him whether he would be appeased if Kasi Raja fell at his feet and apologized for his impudent behaviour. Vishwamitra thought for a while and said he would be satisfied if Kasi Raja fell at his feet and pleaded for his unconditional apology. A joyous Hanuman told Kasi Raja to fall at Viswamitra's feet and Vishwamitra pardoned him. All of them had a hearty laugh when they knew that all this was the prank of Narada.

Hanuman is a living legend who is always engrossed in chanting the Rama Nama. Although he was born in Treta Yuga when Sri Rama had lived, in the Bhagavatha Purana, he is mentioned once or twice at the advent of Sri Krishna in the Dwapara Yuga. He was present at the helm of the flag staff of Arjuna's chariot in the Kurukshetra war. Bhima confronted him when he went to seek the flower Parijatha for Draupadi from the Himalayas. Bhima's pride was subdued by Hanuman. Then we find him in Dwaraka as an instrument in subduing the pride of Balarama, Sathyabhama and Garuda- all the three at the instance of Sri Krishna. Narada was ridiculed by Garuda in the assembly of the Gods and Sathyabhama showed disrespect to Narada. Balarama had become arrogant thinking that he was the most powerful king of Dwaraka belittling Krishna's able presence there. Sri Krishna asked Narada to bring Hanuman to Dwaraka from Kadalivana. Narada sang the glory of Sri Rama and an enticed Hanuman who is attracted to the song followed Narada to Dwaraka. On seeing that he was in a strange place, Hanuman got angry and started destroying the beautiful garden at Dwaraka. He wounded the guards very badly and Balarama instructed Garuda who had come there at that time to overpower the monkey. A great fight ensued between Hanuman and Garuda. Garuda was no match for Hanuman and his wings were broken, legs were fractured and he became unconscious. When Balarama heard the news he was enraged and with a big army he confronted Hanuman. But he was powerless against Hanuman. Balarama was badly injured and he too fell unconscious. Sri Krishna upon hearing the news thought that Hanuman would not recognise him if he went as Sri Krishna. He decided to go as Sri Rama in front of Hanuman. He requested Satyabhama who was imagining herself as the most beautiful and most loved wife of Krishna to become Sita. She dressed herself in dishevelled clothes and unkempt hair as Sita in ashoka vana. On seeing her Krishna rebuked her. Her pride had a great fall. The Lord then requested Rukmini to become Sita. Rukmini prostrated at the feet of the Lord and prayed that if she was a true, devoted and chaste wife of Sri Krishna she may be transformed as Sita. The Lord blessed her and she became Sita.Then that Sri Rama and Sita went to Hanuman who was in the garden and he was overcome with emotion on seeing his most beloved master and his consort.He prostrated at their feet and Krishna as Sri Rama explained to Hanuman that he was born as Sri Rama in Treta Yuga and in this Dwapara Yuga he was born as Sri Krishna.He showed his majestic and all splendid form of Mahavishnu with four arms and Hanuman had the realisation that all are one and the same.He started chanting the Mahamantra from there. "Hare Rama Hare Rama Rama Rama Hare Hare, Hare Krishna Hare Krishna Krishna Krishna Hare Hare." He then departed to Kadalivana his abode. A highly satisfied Krishna revived Balarama and Garuda who apologized to him for their arrogant behaviour and failure to acknowledge the greatness of the Lord Krishna pacified them.

For those who sincerely believe in him, Hanuman is always near at hand. He consoles, protects and pacifies those who take refuge in him. It is told that Mahakavi Tulasidas's Hanuman Chalisa is a very potent tonic even to cure incurable diseases as cancer if recited with a pure heart.

On asking how he considers his relationship with Sri Rama, Hanuman's answer is noteworthy. He says:

"Deha budhyatu Dasosmi, Jeeva budhya
twadamshaka
Atma budhya twamevaham iti me nishchitha mathi"

Meaning: When seen as my body I am your servant or dasa, when seen as jeeva or individual soul I am your part or amsa but when seen as Atma or Supreme, I am yourself.

This is my firm opinion. Hanuman is still believed to be living in the Himalayas all the time chanting the tharaka mantra or Ramanama. He is a living legend and he has received a boon from Lord Sri Rama that he will abandon his mortal body only at the end of the kalpa, and merge with the Supreme. Till then he will be there to protect all those who have taken refuge in Rama. He helps with unseen hands and protects those who have abiding faith in him. His assistance comes from nowhere, when you least believe that some help would come your way. His kindness and large-heartedness is immense. Many are there who will vouchsafe for the long protecting hands Hanuman has rendered them in their hour of need. It is the strength of your belief. All God's ways are strange.

Jai Sri Rambhakt Hanuman

Chapter VII

From Trisha to Nirvaan

Bhagawan says in *The Gita* Chapter 7 Sloka 11:

*Dhrmavirudho bhutheshu kamosmi
Bharatharishabha*

Meaning: Oh, Arjuna, I am desire which is not against righteousness or Dharma. It is said that desire is the root of all evil. Trisha is nothing but desire. But without Trisha or desire there is no action. Every action is centered to fulfil a desire. Desire is not sinful if is not against righteousness. Desire sprouts in the mind from Sankalpa. Sankalpa is imagination or visualization of fulfillment of desire. The noblest desire one can have is to have the craving for salvation or Mukthi. This encourages one to become refined or polished. This desire makes one aware of oneself and to have a grip on oneself. Self-awareness is the basic quality of attaining Mukthi. This means one should be witness to one's own actions. To understand or to realize the witness in one is the ultimate of self-realisation.

For this one has to do practice or upasana or abhyasa or constant endeavour. The whole of *The Bhagavad Gita* is to make one active in the right way.

In Chapter 15 Purushothama Yoga Slokas 3 and 4 Bhagawan says:

*Aswathamenam suviroodhammolam
Asangashasthrena dhridhena chhitwa
Tata param parimargithavyam yasmin gatha na
nivarthandi Bhuyah*

Meaning: Having cut asunder this firm rooted Aswathha tree with the strong axe of non-attachment then that goal should be sought for, going whither, they do not return again.

How to develop non-attachment? One has to have a regular unbroken prayer routine daily which becomes a yagna. This can be five, ten or thirty minutes or even couple of hours and then do other duties unconcerned. Unconcerned does not mean one should be carefree or careless. It only means one should not be unduly concerned with the result of one's actions. Do the duty and leave the result to God. Have God in mind while doing the duty. Daily if one does the chores in this way starting with a prayer one will develop non-attachment by and by. The aswathha tree referred to here is the world we live in. Everyone should have a prayer room in one's own house. It could be a small cubicle even. The significance of having a prayer room is like having a well for pure water in one's house. Water is everywhere but you drink only pure well water. God is everywhere but a prayer room is like a well where you get pure spiritual energy into your system. One can quench the thirst and fill spiritual enegy in one's system.

It is not necessary that one should be a pure vegetarian if one is an aspiring spiritual seeker. The body will accept only what it wants. One should always have a feeling that God is guiding one and we are only an instrument in His hands. Whatever we do, good or bad is His prompting. One should not take credit or feel unduly depressed with the result of an action. Equanimity is the watchword.

The beauty of living is that when one is aspiring for a higher life one is led to the right path, one is shown the right path and answers come one by one. If we are lucky we are led to the Guru who dispels the darkness in our minds. One should have an optimistic approach in everything and see only good in others.

We are makers of our own destiny. Nobody is to be blamed. It is apt to quote this *Doha* from Kabir Das:

Bura jo dhekhane main chlala, Bura na miliya koi
Jo dil khojan apna mujhsa bura na koi

Meaning: I went out in search of a bad one, but could not find any, when I opened my heart and searched there was none as bad as me.

The endeavour for wealth and fulfillment of desire should be through righteous means only. Adherence to Dharma will surely lead to the fourth purushartha i.e. Moksha or salvation or Nirvaan.

The Lord is watching every breath of ours.We have just got to open the door of our heart for Him to enter. It is said if you take one step towards God, God will take ten steps towards you. If Bhagawan is with us, what is there to fear in this world? One should be assured that He is always beside you and then your journey towards the ultimate or Nirvaan will be a roaring success.

May the light of Trisha or desire for Nirvaan kindle in you and may God Almighty show you the safe passage From Trisha to Nirvaan.

May God's blessing be with us all.

Part Two

69

One Act Plays

One

Arjuna's Despondency

Mahabharatha the largest epic in the world, is about the rivalry between kith and kin, the five sons of Pandu, called the Pandavas and the 101 sons of Dhritharashtra, called the Kauravas. The Pandavas and Kauravas are first cousins. The enmity and jealousy reach such a state that war becomes inevitable. Lord Krishna's attempts to settle the issue amicably, by being an emissary of the Pandavas and speaking for them and their right of getting a share of the kingdom, in the assembly of the Kauravas, ends in disaster. Duryodhana, the eldest son of Dhritharashtra, emphatically declares that he would not allow the Pandavas even a space to prick a pin. Thus ensues the battle of Kurukshethra. The battle of good versus evil.

(Krishna has declared that he would not take up arms. He is only Partha's (Arjuna) charioteer. His entire army is fighting in the battle on Duryodhana's side.)

(Here we are in the battle field of Kurukshethra. The great war is about to ensue.)

(The Screen opens—

On stage we find the battle field. Bhishma Duryodhana and Drona are seen on the stage. Duryodhana approaches Acharya Drona and speaks after looking at the Pandava Army.)

Duryodhana: Oh, venerable Sir, look at the large Pandava army arrayed by the son of Drupada, your disciple. Here are mighty bowed heroes, equals of

Bhima and Arjuna. They are all mighty warriors. On our side, we have you, Bhishma Pitamaha, Karna, Kripa, Ashwattama, Vikarna and many other heroes who are willing to sacrifice their lives for my sake in this battle. I believe our army led by Bhishma in insufficient and their army led by Bhima is sufficient. Therefore, all of you standing in your positions, should guard Bhishma Pitamaha.

(Bhishma, who is standing a few feet away, laughs heartily and taking his conch, blows it loudly.
Now Arjuna and Krishna slowly come to the scene in their chariot. They blow their conches. Then beagles and drums are sounded creating tumultuous noise. When the sound dies down-)

Arjuna: Krishna, place the chariot in the middle of the two armies so that I can see who all have come here to wage the battle and die for Duryodhana's cause.

Krishna: Arjuna, see both the armies. Have a look at the entire Battle field.

(Arjuna observes both sides.)

Arjuna: Seeing these kinsmen, Krishna, arrayed to fight, my limbs fail and my mouth is parched. My body quivers. My Gandhiva bow slips from my hand. And my skin burns. My mind is reeling, O Kesava, and I see adverse omens. I see no good in killing kinsmen in battle. I do not desire victory, Krishna nor sovereignty.Of what use is sovrignity to us, O Govinda or enjoyment or life itself? They for whose sake we desire sovrignity and pleasures are gathered here ready to give up life and wealth. Fathers, sons grandsires uncles, fathers–in-law, brothers-in-law and other kinsmen. I do not want to kill them even if they should kill us. No, not even for the sovrignity of the three worlds. O Janardana, by slaying these sons of

Dhritharashtra sin alone will overtake us. How can we be happy by killing our own people? These men with minds of greed see no evil in destroying their family and kin. Why should we be a part of this sin?

(Casting away bow and arrow, Arjuna sits down in the chariot, dejected.)

Krishna: O Brave one, why this infatuation in this hour? Why have you given yourself to this unmanliness and cowardice?

Arjuna: How, O Madhusudana, shall I fight against Bhishma Pitamaha and Acharya Drona who are worthy of respect? Living on alms would be much better rather than killing these noble minded elders.

Krishna: In such a crisis, where comes upon thee, O Arjuna this dejection Un-Aryan Like, disgraceful and contrary to the attainment of heaven? Yield not to unmanliness, O son of Kunthi. It is not worthy of you. Cast off this mean faint-heartedness and arise, O Scorcher of thine enemies.

Arjuna: No, Govinda I cannot fight against my people. Will it not be proper to give up this whole kingdom than shedding the blood of my own relatives and retire to the forest in peace?

Krishna: Do not think that by your high talk of renunciation and retiring to the forest people will adore you and call you brave and intelligent. On the contrary, for centuries to come the blame would be put on you for running away from the battle field. Generation after generation would laugh at you and make fun of your unmanly flight.

Arjuna: O Krishna,I am unable to decide on my further plan of action.I surrender myself at your holy feet.Oh,Lord,Please guide me through this difficult uncertainity as I am your disciple and you are my teacher.

(Arjuna gets down from the chariot and bows down in front of Krishna.)

Krishna: O Arjuna fight the war without thinking of the consequences.Your duty is, and you have the right, only to fight. You do not have control over the outcome.The duty of a person is to do the allotted work as worship to the Lord without expecting any definite fruits thereof.

(Thus ensues *The Bhagavad Gita,* a dialogue between Lord Krishna and Arjuna. It consists of eighteen chapters, where Arjuna puts forth many a question about the goal in life, aim of human birth, about the nature and duty of work about the Self and about the four yogas viz: Gnana Yoga, Raja Yoga, Karma Yoga and Bhakthi Yoga. Lord Krishna answers all the questions. He explains how man can attain true knowledge and then salvation. He also reveals his true Universal Form to Arjuna. Thus *The Gita* is the summary of all knowledge contained in the Vedas and *Upanishads.* In recent times Swami Vivekananda has commented that the Gita exhorts every one of us to arise, awake, and fight our unmanliness so that we emerge active and strong beings. We become true spiritual seekers to realize our true nature and therby do immense good to the world.

Krishna: Are your doubts cleared O Arjuna? Are you freed from the delusory ideas regarding your true nature?

Arjuna: Yes, My Lord. I am grateful to you and am full of bliss with recent realization of true knowledge. My ignorance has vanished. Destoyed is my delusion and I have gained my memory through your grace.My doubts are gone. I will do Thy word.

(Arjuna then stands up, picks up his bow and gets on to the chariot.)

Two

Panchali's Entreaty To Krishna

(When curtain is drawn up, we see Yudhishtira's court in Upaplavya. Yudhishtira and Krishna are seated. Sanjaya enters. Krishna and Yudhishtira welcome him and escort him to a seat.)

Yudhishtira: Oh, Sanjaya, we welcome you. Are Dhrithrashtra and our cousins well? What matter has brought you here?

Sanjaya: Dhritharashtra and your cousins are well. I have come to Upaplavya at the request of Dhritharashtra on a peace mission. Dhritharashtra sends his good wishes and seeks your good will. He wants to see his sons and his brother Pandu's sons living peacefully by avoiding confrontation and war.

Ydhishtira: Oh, Sanjaya, we will be the last to wage a war. We too want peace. We will be satisfied if Duryodhana agrees to part with half of the kingdom and give it to us. You know it is our rightful share.

Sanjaya: Dhritharashtra is willing to give you half of the kingdom. But his sons led by Duryodhana are adamant that they will not part with any part of the kingdom.

Krishna: How can it be tolerated? The Pandavas cannot live on alms and charity for ever. Dhritharashtra should prevail over his son.

Yudhishtira: Although we knew that we were defeated in the game of dice by the cunning of Sakuni, we deemed it to be our lot to go to the forest for twelve long years and one year in cognito just to safeguard dharma. Now we justly request for our share of the kingdom.

Sanjaya: Dhritharashtra very well knows the trials you suffered in the forest and is very sympathetic towards you. But Duryodhana and his brothers cannot be won over. Dhritharashtra wants that there should be no war and peace should prevail. Yudhishtira, what good can there be by killing your kinsmen?

Yudhishtira: As kshatriyas we cannot tolerate injustice. Do you wish that we become beggars for ever just to appease Dhuryodhana? We stand for peace but if we have to fight to redeem our kingdom we are prepared for that. As kshatriyas we don't shirk from our dharma.

Krishna: There is only one course of action left. I will go to Hastinapura as a last resort as your emissary and meet Dhritharashtra and Dhuryodhana and persuade them to see reason. Let me make a last attempt to get your rightful kingdom.

Yudhishtira: Krishna, it would be futile.And I don't want you to jeopardize your life for our sake. Dhryodhana will resort to any means to get rid of you since you are our ally.

Krishna: I am not at all afraid to go to Hastinapura. If they try their dirty tricks on me, I will reduce them to ashes with my infinite powers. But it should be known that we did everything we could to avoid a war. I will go to the extent of asking for five villages for your sake to avoid war. Sanjaya, go back to Hastinapura and inform Dhritharashtra and his sons that I am coming there as the emissary of the Pandavas.

Sanjaya: So be it. I will now take leave of you.

(Sanjaya departs from the scene)

Krishna: Yudhishtira, I will start for Hastinapura tomorrow itself in the company of Satyaki.

Yudhishtira: I will inform the developments to my mother Kunti.

(Yudhishtira leaves the scene and Panchali enters from the other side)

Panchali: Oh, Krishna, what do I hear? I hear that you are going to Hastinapura as the emissary of the Pandavas.

Krishna: Draupadi, what you heard is correct.

Panchali: You are going to beg for five villages for the pandavas and I hear even Bhima and Arjuna are averse to war and want peace.Krishna, if Bhima and Arjuna won't wage a war against the kauravas, my father Drupada, my five sons and the valiant son of Subhadra, Abhimanyu will fight the Kauravas and definitely defeat them.They are impatient to avenge the wrong done and I cannot tolerate the injustice.

Krishna: Be calm, Oh, Draupadi.It is wrong to kill one's own kinsmen in battle.

Panchali: How can I ever be calm, Krishna? You very well know how they dragged me to the open assembly holding me by my hair and tried to disrobe me when my five husbands were helplessly watching.You only saved my honour, Krishna.Yoy should not forget the vow taken by Bhima that he will sever the hand of Dushasana and drink his blood, tearing apart his breast.

Krishna: Have courage Draupadi. Do not be hasty and excited.

Panchali: Krishna, you are the ever powerful all knowing infinite being. Please see these my tresses Krishna. Please see my hair.I have not knotted them since that day.Till I smear them with Dushasana's blood my tresses wiil remain as they are, uncared for and unattended to. Please have mercy O, Madhusudana.

Krishna: Draupadi, fear not.Your solemn vow will be fulfilled.All Dhritharashtra's sons will be slain in war and Dushasana will be killed by Bhima in the bloody battle. It is only a matter of time. I am going to Hastinapura only to declare to the world that we did everything to avoid a war.Dhuryodhana will not relent. War is inevitable.Do not grieve.

Panchali: Krishna, you are all knowing.I am satisfied with your assurance. Thy will be done.

(bows to Krishna and leaves)

Three

Eklavya

(When the curtain is drawn up, we see a thatched house inside the forest. There is a mud statue of Dronacharya underneath a baniyan tree on one side. One can hear the tumultuous noise of barking and howling of dogs and also wailing for two minutes. Then suddenly everything is calm and quiet.)

(Dronacharya with his retinue of disciples namely Bhima, Arjuna, Dharmaputra and some of the Kaurava princess enter. They all are in an agitated mood, with bows and arrows in hand.)

Arjuna: Oh, venerable preceptor Dronacharya, what a terrible thing to happen.All our dogs have been silenced.They are not able to open their mouths.

Dharmaputra: Their mouths have been forcibly shut by arrows deftly shot from a bow. It is a very shameful matter for us.We are princes and have come for hunting and what a turn of events!

Arjuna: What tremendous ability of the archer! He has silenced the dogs without harming them.Only their mouths have been shut.

 Dronacharya: It is true.The one who has sent these arrows is a virtuoso. Such ability is indeed rare.He must be an expert in archery.

(Suddenly Drona sees his statue underneath the baniyan tree and is taken aback.)

Drona: What? How has this my statue come here? Who has kept this statue here? There are flowers and garlands on the statue.

Bhima: There seems to be nobody in this place.

(He calls out: Hey, Hey, Hullo, Hullo... Ekalavya enters with bow and arrows in his hands.Seeing Drona rushes towards him and fully prostrates before him)

Ekalavya: Oh, Great Guru, I am Ekalavya born of low caste parents. I had come to your Ashrama where you were training these princes. I had pleaded with you to make me your disciple and teach me also archery along with these princes. But you had refused to instruct me saying that you teach only Kshathriyas.

Drona: Yes, yes, I remember now. Are you the one who sent the arrows and shut the mouth of the dogs?

Ekalavya: Yes, Holy one. Ever since I returned from your hermitage I have benn practising archery installing this your statue in front of me and dedicating all my prowess at your feet.

Arjuna: But why did you send the arrows on our dogs?

Ekalavya: They were creating hell of a sound and distracting my concentration and practice. I have not harmed or hurt them. I have only made their mouths shut.

Arjuna: (turning to Drona) Oh, Guru, I am afraid this boy has become an invincible person by his prowess in archery.None can defeat him in this profession.

Drona: What you say is true. He has become an adept in this art due to his great Gurubhakthi.

Arjuna: But I beseech you to honour your words.

Drona: What were my words, oh, Arjuna?

Arjuna: You had declared that there will be no one equal to Arjuna in archery.You have to safeguard your words.

Drona: (nodding his head) I remember and I understand.

Arjuna: Please deliberate and do something which will establish me as the greatest archer in the world.

Drona: My words can't become futile. (Thinking for a few seconds he turns to Ekalavya) Oh, Ekalavya, you are the best archer I have ever seen and your dedication and perseverance are commendable. You say you have learnt everything dedicating to me. I want to test your devotion and Gurubhakthi.

Ekalavya: Oh, Lord whatever you say I will accomplish in a minute. Please speak out whatever is in your mind, Sir.

Drona: Ekalavya, the Guru decides when the disciple completes his study. Every disciple, you know, has to render Gurudhakshina after his study is over. I declare that you have completed your study and now I demand my Gurudhakshina.

Ekalavya: Oh, Holy Sir, whatever you ask as Gurudhakshina I am ready to offer you. I will be second to none in service to the Guru. You just name it.

Drona: If you are a worthy disciple cut your right thumb and give it to me as your Gurudhakshina.

(Ekalavya shudders for a moment but recovers and without the least hesitation takes an arrow with a sharp blade at its tip and chops off his right thumb and offers it to his Guru placing it on a leaf. And he fully prostrates befor Drona.)

Drona: (with tears in his eyes helps Ekalavya up and embraces him) Oh Shishya, Your Gurubhakthi, sincerity and devotion will be remembered in three worlds for ever. May you live long and lead a happy and peaceful life. May the infinite God bless you.

.Four

Krishna's Mission

(When curtain is drawn up, we can see Dhritharashtra's and Duryodhana's court in Hastinapura. Dhritharashtra is on the throne. Bhishma, Drona, Karna, Dushasana and many ministers are seated on either side of Dhritharashtra.Duryodhana is seated on his immdediate right side. Krishna, Vidura and Satyaki enter and everybody stand up. Krishna and the other two are received by Dhritharashtra and are given seats and everybody sits down.)

Krishna: Oh, Dhritharashtra and other royal personages of this assembly, I have come here as the emissary of the pandavas. Pandavas do not want to wage a war and destroy their kinsmen. They call for peace. They only seek their rightful share of the kingdom. Dhritharashtra, be kind to the children of Pandu. You must love them as you loved your brother Pandu.

Dhritharashtra: Krishna, I am ever willing to give half of the kingdom to the pandavas.My earnest entreaties to Dhuryodhana is not being listened to.I do not want war and bloodshed.Please try to advice Duryodhana.

Krishna: (turning to Duryodhana) Duryodhana, Please realize that Pandavas are none else than your cousins. They want to live peacefully with you.It is foolishness to wage war. But pandavas are not afraid to take up arms if needed. But why should your entire tribe be destroyed? Please see reason and part with half of the kingdom. The pandavas themselves will install Dhritharashtra on the throne as king and you as heir apparent. Make peace with them.

Bhishma: Do as Govinda says.Make peace with pandavas and avoid war.

Dhritharashtra: If you don't listen to Krishna's advice our race will perish.

Duryodhana: Madhusudana, you wrongly blame me out of your love for the pandavas. The others also blame me.But I am not to be blamed.Pandavas out of their own will staked their kingdom in the play of dice and were defeated. Why should I be blamed for that? Losing the game and their going to the forest was honour bound. For what fault of ours do they now seek battle and wish to slay us? I will not yield to threats. When I was young, my elders did a grievous fault by giving the Pandavas half the kingdom, over which they had no right. But they have lost it at play. I acquiesced then.But now I am not willing to return it to them.

Krishna: (Laughingly) You very well know the play was fraudulently arranged by you in conspiracy with Sakuni.Is it not a grievous wrong you did to Draupadi by dragging her by the hair and trying to disrobe her in the open assembly? You say you have committed no wrong. Did you not try to burn them in the palace of wax? Did you not try to Poison Bhima? And now after having lived twelve years of strife in the forest and one year incognito, you deny them their share of the kingdom. Duryodhana, if you are unwilling to give half the kingdom to pandavas, then give them five states. They will be satisfied with that.

Duryodhana: I am not afraid of war, Krishna. We are not agreeable to give five states.

Krishna: Duryodhana, please see reason and at least give five provinces.

Duryodana: No, Krishna. You needn't ask for five provinces.We will not give it.

Krishna: Then Duryodhana, Pandavas will be satisfied with five villages. Please give five villages to them and avoid war.

Duryodhana: There is no question of any villages; I will not give them.

Krishna: Don't be stubborn, Duryodhana. At least can't you give five houses? They cannot be beggars for ever.

Duryodhana: No, Krishna. I will not part with a place even to prick a pin to the Pandavas. You may advise them to take whatever action they may deem fit.We are ready for war.

Krishna: Adharma has overpowered you. You don't see reason.You have given untold miseries to the pandavas.Don't you see theirs is a righteous cause? You are not willing to part with a place to prick a pin. Duryodhana, dharma has to prevail over adharma. Your tribe will be eraced in the bloody battle. You will sacrifice wantonly your entire people. Beware.

Duryodhana: Dushasana, ask them to bring ropes to tie Madhusudana and torture him. He should be somehow or other made imbecile.Bring ropes. He is Pandavas strongest ally.

(Krishna smiles and reveals his divine Viswarupa)

Dhritharashtra: Oh, Krishna, I can see your infinite divine form through your blessings even though I am blind. But Krishna, I implore you, make me blind again as before. I do not want to see anything else. May this your divine form only remain in my memory always.

(Duryodhana and Dushasana, with ropes in their hands, and the entire assembly swoons.Krishna, after sometime, regains his original form and departs with Vidura and Satyaki on either side of him)

Duryodhana and Dushasana (together): What is this? My head is reeling. I cannot see anything.

Five

Karna's Death

(When the curtain is drawn up, we can see the battle field of Kurukshethra. Karna is trying his best to pull out the wheel of his chariot which is stuck in the mud. Arjuna with bow in hand and Krishna, the charioteer, are near him.)

Karna: It is the curse of the Brahmana, whose cow I unknowingly killed, that has made this wheel of my chariot stuck in the mud. I couldn't remember the mantras necessary to initiate the Brahmastra due to Parasurama's curse. Now I am in this predicament.

Arjuna: Karna, you have benn boasting to everybody that you will kill me in battle. Now you get ready to be killed by me.

Karna: It is not fairplay or dharma in battle to kill one who is unarmed.

Krishna: Ha, Ha, Ha! Oh, Karna, you talk of fairplay now when you are about to be killed. Have you tread the path of righteousness and fairplay when you were a part of a plot when Draupadi was dragged by her hair, insulted dishonoured and disrobed in the open assembly? Did you not ridicule her helplessness? Where were you when the game of dice was played fraudulently and shamelessly and Dharmaputra was cheated? And when Rajamatha Kunti was made to walk barefoot to the forest? Did you not conspire with Duryodhana and administer poison to Bhima? Where was your dharma when you acquiesced to burn the Pandavas and Kuthina in place of wax? And when as per pledge, after completion of twelve years in the forest and one year incognito, grant of kingdom to Yudhishtira was refused? Karna, will you call it chivalry and fairplay when six heroes murdered the tender boy Abhimanyu, who without weapon was fighting with a wheel of his chariot and requested for a fair chance to fight one by one? At those times you conveniently forgot what was dharma, now when you are to be destroyed you talk of fairplay. Arjuna, do not hesitate, send the arrow. The perpetrators of adharma have to be annihilated.

(Arjuna sends a divine arrow and severes the head of Karna. Karna falls down and is in agony. Krishna goes near Karna)

Krishna: Kauntheya, Kauntheya, what is your last wish?

Karna: (in pain) Krishna you are the first one to call me Kunti's son.I wish that my last rites are performed in virgin soil so that the sorrows I suffered in this life may not sprout.

Krishna: It will be done.

Karna: (looking up towards the sky and with folded arms) Oh, Guru and God my father Surya bahgawan, protect me and take me into your fold.

(He breathes his last. Kunti and the other four Pandava princess enter.)

Kunti: Oh, Krishna, I want to see the body of my gallant son.

(Krishna escorts her near the body of Karna. She takes the head in her lap and weeps)

Kunti: How I pleaded with him to join our side in the battle after I told him he was my son (weeps).

Yudhishtira: Oh, Revered Mother, why did you hide the truth of Karna's birth from us? Why did you Mother?

Kunthi: I was unmarried at that time and I was afraid of scandalous talk. When he was born I placed him in a box and left it in the Ganga. A charioteer found the box and brought him up. When he was born he had divine armour and ear pendants.

Arjuna: What a fate it is! I have killed my brave brother.

Krishna: What is fated cannot be blotted. He was true to Duryodhana throughout his life even after knowing that he was Kunthi's eldest son. Such was his attachment and loyalty to Duryodhana. He was true to his friend till his last breath even though he knew he was treading the wrong path. There is nobody in all the three worlds to excel him in charity. When Indra came disguised as Brahmana and begged for his armour he willingly donated it to him even though he knew he would be vulnerable to death without them. Let us salute him.

(Vrushali, Karna's wife enters and walks towards the body of Karna.)

Vrushali: I wish to enter the funeral pyre of my husband. I wish to join him in death as in life.

Krishna: Vrushali, you are a chaste and devoted wife and your wish will be fulfilled. You will join your illustrious husband in death as in life. His life and death will become history and will always be remembered in the three worlds.

(Everybody gathers round the body of Karna and bow
to him)

Six

Kuchela's Redemption

(When curtain is drawn up we see Krishna's Dwaraka Palace. Krishna and Rukmini are relaxing on a diwan)

Krishna: Rukmini, who decides what is in store for people. Nobody is able to foresee the future.

Rukmini: Yes, My Lord. Those who have implicit faith and devotion in you cross the transmigratory cycle with ease.

(Krishna looks far in front of him cupping his hands on his eyes.)

Krishna: Rukmini, today is a great day for me.See who is standing near the gate?

Rukmini: (seeing afar) It is a frail looking old man.

Krishna: I am elated. It is my school mate Kuchela.

(Krishna rushes to the gate through the crowd and in great joy escorts Kuchela to the stage.Krishna embraces him and makes him sit on his own diwan. Rukmini brings water in a vessel.Krishna washes Kuchela's feet and sprinkles the water on his head. When Kuchela is made comfortable Krishna takes the fan from Rukmini's hands and starts fanning him. Kuchela is in a wonder world and looks at everything with utter amazement)

Krishna: Oh, Kuchela. How fortunate that you remembered me! How many years have passed since we studied together in Guru Sandipini's Ashrama learning the Vedas and scriptures.

Kuchela: Yes, yes, O' Lord. It is my utmost good fortune that you recognized me.

Krishna: It is told that meeting of good souls is like taking a holy bath in sacred rivers. Although we are two in body we are one in spirit. Do you remember the many pranks we did together and spent the days in fun and frolic?

Kuchela: The Guru was very kind hearted and generous.

Krishna: Can we forget the day the Guru's wife sent us to bring firewood from the forest and it became late in the evening and there came heavy rains, thunder and lightning. Do you remember we spent the night in a small cave in the forest. The next day a visibly anxious Guru came searching for us and escorted us to the Ashrama. Can we forget that night Kuchela, we were so afraid and scared and how I slept in your lap the whole night?

Kuchela: How can I forget Oh, Lord? That night was horrible, and since you were there I was sure no harm would come to us.

Krishna: Now Kuchela, you must have brought something for me.What is it? What are you hiding under your armpit, Kuchela? Give it to me, give it to me.

(Krishna snatches the small bundle from Kuchela's armpit and opens the Bundle)

Krishna: This is parched rice. Kuchela how thoughtful of you. You must not be shy. People call me the greedy one.

(Krishna eats a handful of the parched rice and was about to have a second helping when Rukmini suddenly catches hold of Krishna's hand.

Rukmini: Oh, Krishna, what are you doing? Don't you have any kindness towards me? Do you want to make me a beggar? Half of your wealth has gone to Kuchela already by your eating one handful of rice. Don't make me a baggar woman by eating the whole thing, You, who know everything.

Krishna: Rukmini, yes, yes, I understand. You caught hold of my hand at the right time. I forget everything when my eyes fall on my devotees.Kuchela had eaten my share of rice which the Guru's wife had given him when we were in the Ashrama. All his misery is over today. He is a great devotee and friend of mine. I will do anything to help my bhakthas.

(Krishna turns to Kuchela who is almost drowsing and not aware of what is going on)

Krishna: Kuchela, have you been happy and comfortable here?

Kuchela: I am the most fortunate man in the world today. I could meet you and talk to you.I am overwhelmed by your hospitality. Krishna, I do not seek anything I need only your blessings.Let me take leave of you now.Parting with you is always painful.But let me go. I am most happy and joyful. I have only one request Krishna, let my mind always think about you. Let my ears always hear your stories and my eyes fall on your splendid form.Let my hands worship you always and my feet travel to holy places where you reside. Krishna, let me have infinite devotion and Bhakthi in you

Krishna: All your wishes will always be fulfilled. Go peacefully now; remember me always. May you ever remain joyful and happy.

(Kuchela slowly leaves the scene with Krishna escorting him)

A Short Story

Work Is Worship

Ever since Bittu, his fourth son, brought his newly married wife to his house, Gopal Sharma was a bit anxious. Shalini was a beautiful lass but lacked the competence of a disciplined house wife.Like the other three sons' wives she loved a luxurious life and never cared to use her hands in household chores.She loved beautifying herself in front of the mirror, passing her fingers through her long tresses admiring its beauty. There were numerous concoctions of facial and skin lotions on her dressing table and any new advertisement in the T.V. for any new beautifying product would definitely find a place among the various bottles and containers on her table. Sharmaji was really worried. He was not much affluent and the profits he gained from his business was only sufficient to be squandered away by these his sons' wives. They never cared to be thrifty and although he was no miser, Sharmaji felt there was much to be desired in the way his daughters-in- law handled the matters in the household. He was remorse and sad as he thought about his dear Rukmini who had left him five years back for her heavenly abode. She was efficient, dexterous, kind and loving and thinking about her Sharmaji sighed heavily. As he took off his shirt and put it on the hanger, he felt thirsty. The summer was intense and he had perspired much walking from his shop to his house. His call for a glass of water seemed to have fallen on deaf ears and very reluctantly he started walking to the kitchen side, when old and faithful Meena, the maid servant, was seen walking towards him, water in hand.

"Where are all my daughters?" asked Sharmaji.

"They are all busy with their own works. One is listening to the CD she bought yesterday. The other is trying out the sari she bought yesterday. Gopika is with her ornaments as usual and Shalini is having her bath," answered Meena.

"What is it that the cook is making for lunch today?" asked Sharmaji.

"Sir, Radha says her husband likes only phoolgobi. So she has asked for Gobi vegetable curry. Gomathi's husband likes green leaves and so she sent Mathang to market to bring fresh greenleaves. Gopika wants something with paneer for her husband and since Shalini got up late she has not instructed the cook yet," said Meena. "And we have chappathis, rice and naan," added Meena. Sharmaji had a disgruntled look on his face. "My God, where will all this end?" he said. Meena brought out the topic of the washer woman who had asked for a loan of five hundred rupees. Sharmaji became angry and said, "I cannot go on giving loans to everybody." He walked off to his room and lay down on his bed.

He was unduly worried as he thought over the dwindling income he was having from his business. He was a wholesale plastic goods merchant. The markets had become dull due to recession and the retailers were delaying to clear the bills. Every where there was a gloomy outlook and his creditors were insisting on prompt payments. Three thousand rupees to the washerwoman every month, eight thousand to the cook, five thousand for the maid washing the utensils and sweeping the floor, two thousand to Mathang and five thousand to Meena. Where will all this end? Apart from this, there were monthly grocery expenses, milk expenses and daily expenses. Whew! If only Rukmini were alive! When she was there she had only Meena to assist her. How deftly she used to manage all the matters!

Trouble started when his sons started getting married and Rukmini expired.She had breast cancer. She didn't want anybody to know she was suffering. She endured the pain silently and when he came to know it was too late. What a fate!

Radha, when she came, she was supple.She couldn't do heavy work.The arrival of Gomathi made things worse.There were frequent quarrels between them as to who will do what work.Gopika was shrewd.She avoided all work and cunningly made Sharmaji employ a cook, a washerwoman an errand boy and a maid, apart from Meena, to wash the vessels and sweep the floor.How the expenses mounted? Shalini, the new one, was no better. Sharmaji wondered what would happen if Mohan, his fifth son, also got married. God, save me!

Sharmaji was regular in his prayers. Daily after his ablution he would sit in front of his household deity and recite prayers for about 45 minutes. He would then read the scriptures.Breakfast would be taken after that and he would go to his shop. He would come back from his shop at about 8.30p.m,have his bath and meditate for about 20 minutes light the arathi and then have his dinner.He was pained that none of his sons' wives did her prayers to the Deity.What to do? Everybody had their own ways.He would have been happy if any of them had lit the lamp in the morning and at least said a few prayers.But it was not to be.

Among his sons, only Mohan was different.He had inculcated the habit of saying his prayers from his parents.Rukmini was very religious minded and although she had trained their sons to say prayers when they were children, as they grew up they abandoned the habit except Mohan.Sharmaji never saw any of the others pray or never knew if they ever did any prayers.He was happy that at least one of his sons was following his line and after his demise there would be at least one to keep up the family tradition and belief and to offer arathi to the deity.

Mohan was different from the other four and although after his graduation Sharmaji wanted him to join his business, he politely declined.Due to his single minded perseverance he secured a job as a clerk in one of the banks in the town. As the job rotation took place Mohan was assigned the cashier's duty.There was some rush in the bank one day and Mohan was busy handing over cash to the customers.As he raised his head suddenly his eyes fell on a comely girl in the savings Bank counter.Mohan's heart gave a jump and his concentration was a bit disturbed in handing over the cash. He would with one eye see what and where the girl was doing and as she approached the cash counter his heart missed a beat. As he called the number 17, the token number, the girl came in front of the cash counter and gave him the token.In his excitement he asked her what was her amount and she replied it was two thousand five hundred. Mohan noted the name signed on the back of the cheque. "Gita".His mind started wandering and instead of giving five five hundred rupee notes he handed over seven.He noted the denomination correctly as 7x 500 on the reverse of the cheque.The girl too felt a bit shaken when Mohan stared at her and handed over the cash.She forgot to count the cash, put the passbook and cash in her hand bag and left the premises abruptly.

In the evening it was time to tally the cash and suddenly Mohan found that his cash balance was short by rupees one thousand. Panic seized him.This had not happened to him ever before. He asked for the bunch of paid cheques and withdrawal slips and started checking the denominations on the back of the instruments. As he turned one of the instruments he found he had given one thousand rupees more to the customer.Instead of giving five five hundred rupee notes he had given seven.And the name started clearly ringing in his mind. "Gita". He checked the account number and details of the customer and the address. He asked permission from the manager to go out for 15 minutes and taking his scooter he went to the address.When he rang the bell, an elderly gentleman opened the door. He asked him whether he was Mr.Narasimhan and explained the reason for his coming there that he had inadvertently handed over seven five hundred rupee notes instead of five to the bearer, a girl, of the instrument.Immediately Mr.Narasimhan called his daughter Gita and asked her to bring the cash. She came running with the handbag and told them she had not removed the cash from the handbag and it was intact.Her father did not tell her anything. She took out the cash and passbook and handed over to Mohan asking him to check. Mohan counted and showed them that there were seven notes instead of five. Both Mohan and Gita were most apologetic to each other.They repeatedly expressed their sorrow at the fault but Mohan, who had although recovered the rupees one thousand excess paid, had lost his heart there in Narasimhan's residence.Mr.Narasimhan was happy to know he was the cashier at the bank and he offered him a cup of coffee which Mohan politely refused. Mohan felt some reluctancy in leaving the place as his mind was on Gita.From their short conversation he knew she was doing her final year B.A. in the Womens' College nearby.

After going home that day his mind wouldn't rest.Mohan had a disturbed sleep.Early morning he got up. After his bath he was at his prayers and his concentration was on that beautiful lovely face of Gita. However much he tried to concentrate his mind would come back to Gita. He knew there was a temple near Shukrawarpet where Gita's house was situated.He decided to go to the temple there.Entering the shrine, he prayed to the deity to enble him to realize his wish of seeing Gita once more although he was feeling a bit guilty about his wish. He made three slow circumambulations of the temple in the fond hope that he would meet her. Failing to behold her, he returned crestfallen to his home. He was not to be disheartened. He had the fond hope that God would definitely fulfil his wish and so he started to go to that temple daily. He changed the timing and on the fourth day he went to the temple at 6.00 a.m. As he prayed to the deity and came out of the shrine, he beheld Gita entering the temple with an elderly woman who must have been her mother. His joy knew no bounds and as he passed them her eyes too fell on him. He said "Hello" and wished her Good Morning. Her mother asked her who he was and she told her he was the cashier in the bank. He made pranams to her mother and his eyes were constantly on them as he made the circumambulation. But somehow or other he lost track of them and he returned home. Anyway he was glad God had fulfilled his wish. So next day he went to the temple sharp at 6.00 a.m. anxious whether he would meet her again. As he parked the scooter and was about to enter the gate to his amazement he found her too entering the gate but without anybody escorting her. With quick steps he hastened to her side and greeted her. She too seemed to be happy to meet him. He asked her whether she came regularly to the temple and she answered in the affirmative. From their conversation that day he knew she was studying for English Literature and her passions and ambitions in life. And so the friendship grew.

Among his sisters–in- law, Mohan liked Shalini the best. She was playful to him and would often tease him on one count or other. When she came to know that he was going to the temple regularly in the mornings she questioned him on his intentions and she knew there must be something in the offing.Her persistant taunts made him let the cat out of the bag. He told her he was going not only to pray but to meet a girl whom he very much wanted to bring to the household as his dear wife. There started an elaborate description of how charming and beautiful the girl was but Shalini interrupted him and told him she would go to the temple with him the next day to have a first hand sight of his beloved. So they went sister-in-law and brother-in-law next day to the temple sharp at 6.00 a.m. in his scooter. They said their prayers and waited for Gita outside and soon she came in her beautiful stride along with her mother.They waited till they came out of the shrine after their prayers and soon Mohan introduced Gita and her mother to Shalini.Her mother was most courteous and invited them to their house which was nearby and Shalini was only too happy to visit their house and know more about Gita and her parents.Mr.Narasimhan had only three more years to retire from L.I.C. where he was an assistant manager. His jovial demeanour was much appreciated by Shalini and after pleasantries and a cup of coffee, Mohan and Shalini returned to their home.Mohan was after Shalini to somehow get his father's consent. Bhittu was not serious when Shalini told him about Mohan's affair.He only made some passing jokes saying he was too small to get married.When all the daughters-in-law were together in the dining room gossiping after the menfolk had left, Shalini let the cat out of the bag. Radha and Gopika were not much concerned with the news but Gomathi had doubts whether they were affluent enough to become their close relatives especially because Gita's father was only an assistant manager. She doubted whether Gita's upbringing was worthy enough to make one equal to them. But Shalini was insisting that she was a comely girl suitable for Mohan and the most important thing was Mohan adored her.

That night as Sharmaji completed his meditation and prayers he was served his special delicacies and Sharmaji was in good mood after dinner. Shalini had arranged with the cook to serve Sharmaji his favourite dishes. Sharmaji relaxed in his chair and Radha, Gomathi and Shalini were near him. His eldest son, Srini, was reading the newspaper and Subbu, the second son, was narrating to Pappa about the day's development in the business front. Sharmaji relaxed. Radha prepared a delicious pan and served it personally to her father-in-law. After an interval, Shalini addressed Pappaji and told him that Mohan was attaining the age of marriage. He was also desirous of getting married. Mohan had expressed his desire to her. Sharmaji was fond of his youngest son and he smiled and did not utter anything. His silence was encouragement to Shalini and she boldly told Pappaji that they needn't have the trouble of running around for a girl as Mohan himself had found his girl. Sharmaji became curious and so Shalini explained to him all the details about the girl and her father.She also suggested that it would be only right on Pappaji's part to meet Mr.Narasimhan and request for his consent. Sharmaji told them that he would go to Narasimhan's house next Sunday.

Over a cup of coffee Sharmaji explained the purpose of his visit to Mr.Narasimhan. Narasimhan was only too happy to hear the request. He told Sharmaji that Gita was his only daughter and he was agreeable if she consented. Narasimhan informed that he would let him know their decision in a week's time.Mr.Narasimhan after consulting his daughter and after making discreet enquiries at the bank gave his assent for the marriage, but insisted that the marriage could be conducted only after Gita's final exams which were due in April. Another four months were left for both the families to prepare for the wedding ceremony. Sharmaji did not insist on a very large dowry but Mr. Narasimhan assured a hundred sovereigns and Fifty thousand in cash. Radha and Gomathi coaxed Pappaji to ask for more but Sharmaji was not a greedy person and not to be tempted. He was satisfied with what Mr. Narasimhan offered. Moreover he himself had a personal liking for the girl.

With the more than abundant blessings from the parents, friends and relatives the wedding was conducted in a befitting manner.Gita was a smart and simple girl who was brought up well and she had winning ways with everyone and everything she undertook. Soon she won everybody's heart. She would get up at 5.00 a.m. in the morning and light the lamp before the household deity. After that she would have her bath and in the process clean the toilet and bathroom. Then she would chant the prayers that her mother had taught her and spend sometime in the prayer room. Then she would go to the kitchen and assist Meena and the cook in preparing the day's dishes. From Meena, she gathered the favourite dishes of each and everyone in the household. She would go to the market personally and buy all the vegetables and other requisite things necessary in the kitchen. So much so Sharmaji was able to dispense with the services of Mathang the errand boy. When Radha knew that Gita was coming to the kitchen early, she also started getting up early and came to the kitchen. She found Gita doing arathi early in the morning in the deity's room and something made her heart gladden and she too started to do her prayers in whatever way she knew along with Gita. When Gopika and Shalini knew that Radha and Gita were in the kitchen early in the morning, they decided to join in helping in the kitchen work. Gomathi was a hard nut to crack but she reluctantly made her way to the kitchen and started rendering help. When all were there, Gita told the cook that she would try her hand at cooking and soon she started making dishes which were relished by everyone in the family. Radha and Shalini were not to be left behind. They tried out various dishes they knew and soon Gomathi and Gopika joined, with the result that there was no need for a cook and he was given his dues and sent away. Gita, being intelligent and vivacious, nobody felt bored or tired in doing the kitchen work. Everybody gathered round her and the day's work was accomplished happily and peacefully. Gita would sing Bhajans when she was doing the work and the kitchen would reverberate with her melodious sound. When the other four started to prepare the daily dishes Gita said there were too many cooks and she started cleaning the utensils ,plates and pots.Soon Shalini joined her in her chores. Gomathi was not content just to watch the fun and she too joined. Gita then started sweeping and wiping the floor. She would always be singing or talking pleasant talk while doing her job and Shalini and Gomathi helped her in executing the tasks. Soon the maid who was engaged in sweeping and wiping the floor was sent off. Gita now found that there was ample time still left. She detested to sit idle. She started washing the clothes. When Shalini and Gomathi saw her washing the clothes on the washing stone, they asked her what she was upto. She said she didn't like sitting idle, an idle mind was devil's workshop. She liked to work and that would provide vigour and vitality to her health. Her mother had trained her to do whatever work was there in the house. She considered each work as an offering to god. No work was mean to her. She found pleasure and joy in accomplishing any task. Gomathi and Shalini were amazed at her dedication and attitude to work. They shed their ego to some extent and joined in washing the clothes. Soon the washer woman was paid off and sent away

And this was the way the five ladies started managing the household on their own. Gita was very alert to see that no quarrel or bitterness erupted among the ladies and she was there taking care of everything and rendering help wherever needed. Sharmaji was the happiest man.There was no loose talk in the household and everybody was sharing the burden with each other and everyone was ready to help the other.Moreover early in the morning in Sharmaji's house you could hear all the members in the family together chanting and singing prayers and at the end of the prayers Sharmaji would offer arathi to the deity. So the proverb says "A family that prays together stays together."

About the Author

Mr. Mukundan Menon

Born on 19th of January, 1951 in Kedah, Malaysia, Mukundan Menon had his school education from National High School, Irinjalakuda, Kerala (India). A scholar throughout his academic life, Mukundan was also an exponent of Kathakali, Folk dance and Ottanthullal. A first class graduate in Physics, he remains indebted to Christ College and its founder Principal Fr. Gabriel for his spectacular achievements. An outstanding sportsman Mukundan had secured three university-titles in Badminton and Tennis and a gold-medal in English when he passed out from the college. He had been a Bank executive for twenty-eight years and had opted for voluntary retirement in December, 2000.

Mukundan loves to read *The Bible* on Sundays, *The Quran* on Fridays and *The Nitnem* on Thursdays. *The Ramayana*, *The Geeta*, and the gospels of Sri Ramakrishna are read daily. He has been studying *The Geeta* since the age of twenty-one. Mukundan's maiden book *At Thy Feet* comprising of a collection of poems, articles, and a short autobiographical sketch was published in 2008. *Pushpanjali*, a book in Malayalam-language consisting of four novelettes, was also published in the same year. *Read Yourself To Immortality*, a spiritual adventure was published in 2010. Mukundan has been the author of many short stories, articles and poems. He strongly believes that humanity is heading towards enlightenment within the next 100 years. Two of his significant articles are: *Why I Pray* (published in *White Line Journal*), and *The Pigeon's Prayer* (published in *Bhavan's Journal*).

Address: T. Mukundan Menon

BG- 2, Soorya Sobha Apartments

Chirakkad, Kunnathurmedu

Palakkad – 678 013

Kerala, India.

E-mail :   remamukund77@yahoo.co.in

Phone   :   + 91 9846508206

www.ingramcontent.com/pod-product-compliance
Lightning Source LLC
LaVergne TN
LVHW041721190726
843493LV00007B/2184